Contents

To the student

1 In this book you will learn and practise the language you need to do most simple writing tasks – writing letters, telegrams and telexes, reports, etc.

2 Read the instructions carefully. If you do not understand, ask your teacher to explain.

3 Your teacher is there to help you to learn. If you have problems discuss them with him or her.

4 If you work with other students in your group you can help each other to learn more. Co-operate with the other students. Help them and ask them to help you.

A Filling in forms

Look at the two forms and discuss them with your teacher:

This is Tony. He likes acting and he wants to join the Bradford Theatre Group.

1

Bradford Theatre Group – Application Form

Please write in BLOCK CAPITALS

Surname ___FIELD___   Title Mr/~~Mrs~~/~~Miss~~/~~Ms~~*

First Names ___ANTHONY JAMES___

Home Address ___'CRAIGMILLS' WOODPARK LANE___

Town ___GLANTREE___

County ___FIFE , SCOTLAND___

Postcode ___GF3 4PY___   Telephone ___6941783___

Present Address ___753 , HIGH STREET___

Town ___BRADFORD___

County ___YORKS, ENGLAND___

Postcode ___BD1 7GD___   Telephone ___212890___

Age ___28___ Sex ___M___ Occupation ___STUDENT___

Date of Birth ___9th AUGUST 19--___ Place of Birth ___GLANTREE___

Nationality ___BRITISH___   Marital Status ___MARRIED___

Interests ___THEATRE , CINEMA , READING___

I would like to become a member of the Bradford Theatre Group and I enclose my subscription of £3.00.

Signature ___A J Field___   Date ___24/4/--___

* Delete as applicable.

PENGUIN ELEMENTARY
WRITING SKILLS

Anne Parry, Sharon Hartle and Mark Bartram

ELT

PENGUIN BOOKS

Published by the Penguin Group
27 Wrights Lane, London W8 5TZ, England
Viking Penguin Inc., 40 West 23rd Street, New York, New York 10010, USA
Penguin Books Australia Ltd, Ringwood, Victoria, Australia
Penguin Books Canada Ltd, 2801 John Street, Markham, Ontario, Canada L3R 1B4
Penguin Books (NZ) Ltd, 182–190 Wairau Road, Auckland 10, New Zealand

Penguin Books Ltd, Registered Offices: Harmondsworth, Middlesex, England

First published 1989

Edited by Michael Nation

Designed by Mike Brain

Illustrated by Helen Charlton

Filmset in Malaysia

Made and printed in Great Britain by Hazell, Watson & Viney Ltd,
Member of BPCC plc,
Aylesbury, Bucks

Roundhay Health Club – Application Form

Family Name __MARSHALL__ (BLOCK CAPITALS)

Other Names __Anne__

Mr/Mrs/Miss/<u>Ms</u> (Underline as appropriate.)

Age __23__ Sex __F__ Marital Status __Single__

Nationality __British__

Occupation __Bicycle Mechanic__

Full Address __23 Oak Street__

Town __Leeds__

County __Yorkshire__

Postcode __LS3 6BW__ Telephone __0995-914241__

Name and address of family doctor __Dr Finsworth__

__4, Brown Road, Leeds__

Sports __Swimming, tennis, skiing__

Interests __Travelling, cooking__

I would like to join the Roundhay Health Club. I am in good
health and I enclose my subscription of £10 cash/~~cheque~~*

Signature __Anne Marshall__ . Date __24|4|--__

* Delete as appropriate.

2 This is Anne. She loves
sports and she wants to join
the Roundhay Health Club.

3 Now complete the paragraphs, using the information from the forms. The numbered list underneath the text will tell you what kind of word is needed. The first one is done for you.

a Tony Field is a (1) _student_ from (2) _____. He is (3) _____, (4) _____ and he lives in (5) _____. He was born in (6) _____ on the (7) _____. He wants to join the (8) _____ and he likes (9) _____, _____ and _____.

1 Occupation
2 Country (see home address)
3 Age
4 Marital Status
5 Town (see present address)
6 Place of Birth
7 Date of Birth
8 Name of theatre group
9 Interests

b Anne Marshall is (1) _23_ years old. She is a (2) _____ from (3) _____. She wants to join the (4) _____. Her doctor's name is (5) _____. She is in good health and she enjoys (6) _____, _____ and _____. She also likes (7) _____ and _____.

1 Age
2 Occupation
3 Town (see Full Address)
4 Name of Health Club
5 Doctor's name
6 Sports
7 Interests

B Titles in English

1

Men/Boys	Mr
Married women	Mrs or Ms
Single women/Girls	Miss or Ms
Doctors	Dr

Mrs and Miss are the traditional titles. Many women and girls now prefer the title Ms. They do not think it is important to say if they are married or not.

What is your title? _____

2 Anne Marshall likes the title 'Ms'.

Look at this:

Mr/Mrs/Miss/Ms	Underline as appropriate.
~~Mr/Mrs/Miss~~/Ms	Delete as applicable.
Mr/Mrs/Miss/(Ms)	Circle as appropriate.
Mr ☐ Mrs ☐ Miss ☐ Ms ☑	Tick as applicable.

3 Now complete the details about yourself:

Title:	Mr/Mrs/Miss/Ms	*Delete as applicable.*
Age Group:	Under 21 ☐	*Tick as appropriate.*
	21–30 ☐	
	31–50 ☐	
	Above 50 ☐	
Sex:	M F	*Circle as appropriate.*
Marital Status:	Married/Single/Divorced/Widowed	*Underline as appropriate.*

4 The title in English is used only with a surname.

We can say	Ms Marshall
or	Anne
or	Ms Anne Marshall
but not	Ms Anne

Your name is _____ title and surname

or _____ first name

C Punctuation

1 Look:

,	comma
.	full stop
?	question mark
'	apostrophe
ABC	capital letters
abc	small letters

2 Look at the punctuation in this passage:

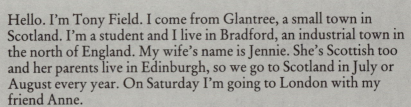

> Hello. I'm Tony Field. I come from Glantree, a small town in Scotland. I'm a student and I live in Bradford, an industrial town in the north of England. My wife's name is Jennie. She's Scottish too and her parents live in Edinburgh, so we go to Scotland in July or August every year. On Saturday I'm going to London with my friend Anne.
> What's your name? Where do you live?

3 Discuss with your partner and your teacher:

a When do we use capital letters in English?
b When do we use full stops?
c When do we use apostrophes?
d When do we use question marks?
e When do we use commas?

4 Now write out this passage using the correct punctuation:

> hello i m anne marshall i live in leeds a large town in the north of england near bradford i like travelling and on saturday i m going to london with tony who is tony well he s my scottish friend he s married and his wife s name is jennie

D Filling in a form

Now fill in the form on the next page for yourself or for your partner:

Balmy Holiday Club – Application Form

Surname _____ (BLOCK CAPITALS) Mr/Mrs/Miss/Ms*

Other Names _____ Sex _____

Date of Birth _____ Place of Birth _____

Marital Status _____ Occupation _____

Home Address _____ Postcode _____

_____ Tel. No. _____

Office Address _____

_____ Tel. No. _____

*Delete as applicable

Please tick (√) as appropriate:

SPORTS	Yes	No	DIET	Yes	No
Can you swim?			Do you like British food?		
Can you windsurf?			Do you like French food?		
Can you ride a bicycle?			Do you like Italian food?		
Can you play tennis?			Do you like Indian food?		
			Do you like Chinese food?		

or complete: 'I like _____ food'

TRAVEL

Where would you like to go? (Tick (√) as appropriate.)

The Far East	☐	Russia	☐
South America	☐	China	☐
The Middle East	☐	North America	☐
Africa	☐	European countries	☐

Others _____

I would like to join the Balmy Holiday Club. I enclose £2.00 cash/cheque.*

Signature _____ Date _____

*Delete as applicable.

UNIT 2

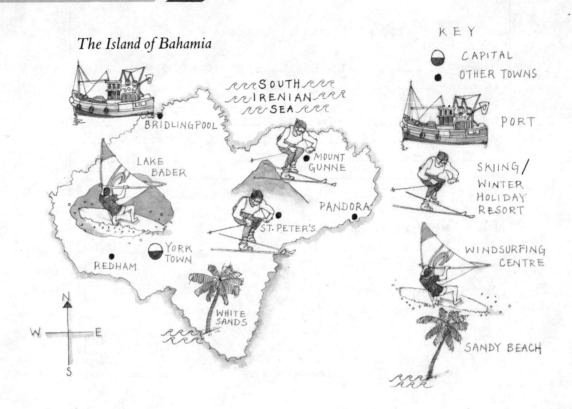

The Island of Bahamia

KEY

CAPITAL
OTHER TOWNS

PORT

SKIING /
WINTER
HOLIDAY
RESORT

WINDSURFING
CENTRE

SANDY BEACH

SOUTH
IRENIAN
SEA

BRIDLINGPOOL

LAKE
BADER

MOUNT
GUNNE

PANDORA

ST. PETER'S

REDHAM

YORK
TOWN

WHITE
SANDS

N
W   E
S

A Location

1 Match the names of the places on the map with the correct description
below. Then write the names in your exercise book. The first one is
done for you:

a A large port in the north of the island. _____*Bridlingpool.*_____
b A small town near the capital.
c A sandy beach on the south coast.
d The capital of Bahamia, south of Lake Bader.
e A holiday island in the Irenian Sea.
f An important skiing centre.
g A popular wind-surfing centre north of York Town.
h A winter holiday resort south of Mount Gunne.
i A seaside town in the east of the island.

2 Now write eight sentences about the island of Bahamia, like this:

Example:
a This is Bridlingpool, a large port in the north of the island.

3 Prepositions and articles

Look at these examples:

Sicily is **an island in the** Mediterranean Sea.

Palermo is **the** capital.

Monreale is **a** small town **near the** capital.

San Vito is **a** sandy beach **on the** north coast.

Taormina is **a** holiday resort **north east of** Mount Etna.

Messina is **a** large port **in the north east of the** island.

The Platani and **the** Salso are rivers **in the** south **of the** island.

Now circle the correct words in these sentences.
The first one is done for you.

Edinburgh is | —
a
an
(the) | capital of Scotland. The Highlands are | —
a
an
the

mountains | from
at
in
by | the north of Scotland.

Liverpool is | —
a
an
the | famous port | in
at
on
to | the west coast of England

and Hoylake is | —
a
an
the | seaside town south | on
of
from
at | Liverpool.

Leeds is | —
a
an
the | industrial city | on
in
near
at | the north of England.

London is | —
a
an
the | capital of England and Croydon is a town

on
from
near
at | London. The Isle of Wight is | —
a
an
the | island in the English Channel.

4 Exchange books with your partner. Complete the diagram below. Invent and write in the names of the capital, some different towns, mountains, lakes etc. Write in the name of the island and the sea.

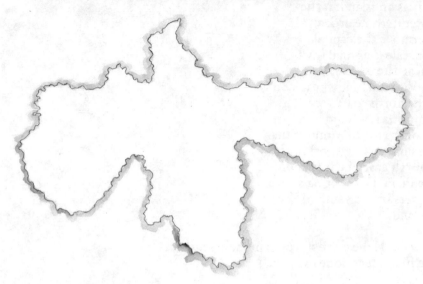

Exchange books again. Write a description of the island your partner has named. Begin like this:

_____ *is an island . . .*

B Family

The Cartenian Royal Family

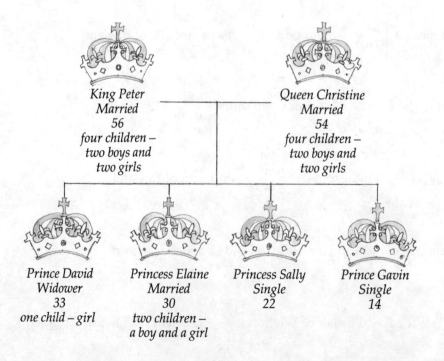

King Peter
Married
56
four children –
two boys and
two girls

Queen Christine
Married
54
four children –
two boys and
two girls

Prince David
Widower
33
one child – girl

Princess Elaine
Married
30
two children –
a boy and a girl

Princess Sally
Single
22

Prince Gavin
Single
14

1 Look at the Cartenian Royal Family and correct these sentences. In every sentence the *name* is correct. For example:

a *King Christine is single and has no children.*
You write:

Queen Christine is married and has four children, two boys and two girls.

b Prince Peter is 83. He is divorced and has 83 children.
c King Sally is 42. She is married and has no children.
d Queen Elaine is seven. She is single and has no children.
e Princess Christine is 26. She is married and has a baby.
f King David is 30. He is a widower and has no children.
g Princess Gavin is 20. He is married and has two children, a boy and a girl.

C Introducing yourself

Hello. I'm Richard. I'm 28. I live in Bradford and I'm married. I've got two children. I'm a photographer for 'Wildlife' magazine. I like travelling, swimming and tennis and I want to go to Bahamia this summer.

Now write about yourself in the same way. Start like this:
Hello, I'm ...

2 Read this description of Gary:

This is Gary. He is 24. He lives in Pandora and he is single. He has no children. He is a disc-jockey at the Feathers Club. He likes pop-music and riding his motor-bike. He wants to find a girlfriend this summer.

Compare the descriptions of Richard and Gary. What changes do we make when we use 'he' or 'she' instead of 'I'? Discuss these changes with your teacher.

3 Activity

Copy this form onto a piece of paper. Fill it in with information about yourself. Do not write your name. You are Jan Mystery.

Balmy Holiday Club – Registration Form

Name: Jan Mystery

Date of Birth:

Address:

Age:

Marital Status:

Occupation:

Children:

Interests/Hobbies:

Brothers and Sisters:

Height:

Hair Colour:

Favourite popstar:

Left-handed/Right-handed:

Fold your paper and put it in your teacher's box or bag.

Now take out a piece of paper, open it and read the information. Try to decide which student this describes. Write a description with the correct name. Look at the description of Gary on page 13 before you start. Begin like this:

I think this is (name of student). $\begin{matrix} He \\ She \end{matrix}$ *is* _____ *years old* _____.

Now give your description to the student.

4 Now write a description of the most interesting person you know – not yourself! Invent the details if you want.

D Informal letters

1 Read the letter and answer these questions:

   a Who is the letter from?
   b Where does the writer live?
   c Who is it to?
   d Why is she writing?

> 23 Oak Street
> LEEDS
> LS3 6BW.
>
> 9th April 19--
>
> Dear Gary,
> I got your address from the Balmy Holiday Club Penfriend Association. I was in Bahamia on holiday last summer and I like the island very much - especially your town, Pandora.
> I live in Leeds, a large town in the north of England. People from the south don't like it because it's industrial, but the people are friendly and I'm happy here.
> I'm 23 years old and I'm single. I work as a bicycle mechanic for Northern Bikes, a small company near my house. I'd like to write to you and perhaps exchange visits. Please write if you are interested.
>
> With best wishes,
>
> Anne (Marshall)

2 Look at the letter above. Complete the text below:

   Anne Marshall is from _____, a _____ town _____ the _____ of England. She likes _____ very much. She was there on holiday last _____.

   She is _____ years old and she is _____. She works as a _____ for _____, a small company near her _____.

   She is writing to _____, who lives in _____, a seaside town on the north-east coast of _____.

3 Informal letter layout

Look at how we usually set out an informal letter:

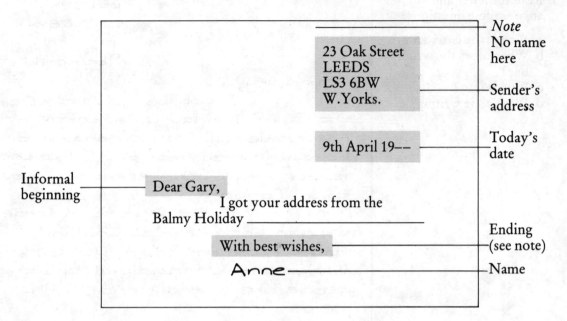

NOTE The most common ways of ending an informal letter are:

OR

OR

'Love' and 'With love' are usually used when writing to members of your family or good friends. For less familiar endings people prefer 'Regards' or 'Yours'.

BAHAMIAN HERALD

12th April

PEN-FRIENDS

FINNISH woman, 35, wants to write to interesting student of English. Interests: cooking, swimming and anthropology. Please write to: Ingrid Kytomaa, Box 3820

JAPANESE teenager would like pen-friend to exchange letters in English. Hobbies: pop-music, football, stamp-collecting. Write to: Yoshiro Fukona, Box 7891

PORTUGUESE photographer, 28, is looking for pen-friend to write letters in English and perhaps exchange visits. Write to Jorge Camoes, Box 3821

Choose *one* of these pen-friend advertisements and write a letter to the person. Your letter must be correctly set out. Look at the layout on page 16 and the letter on page 15 for help.

A Formal letters

1 Read the advertisement and answer this question:

What can you do with Balmy Holidays?

ESCAPE WITH BALMY HOLIDAYS!

Tired of the rain and cold? Then come with us to a Tropical Paradise. Swimming, scuba diving, luxury accommodation.

Or ride a camel across the Sahara, safari in Kenya or go skiing in summer in Argentina. The impossible is possible with Balmy Holidays, and at a very reasonable price.

Contact:
James Hines,
Balmy Holidays,
24 Eastwood Street,
London NW4

2 Addresses

In English we start a formal letter like this:

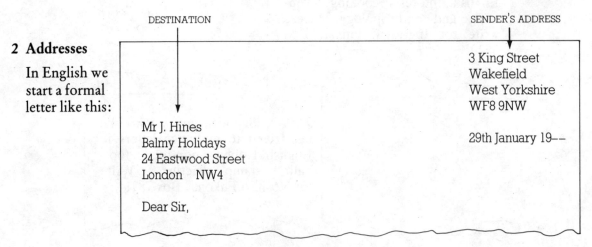

DESTINATION

SENDER'S ADDRESS

3 King Street
Wakefield
West Yorkshire
WF8 9NW

29th January 19‒‒

Mr J. Hines
Balmy Holidays
24 Eastwood Street
London   NW4

Dear Sir,

3 Punctuation

Look at the capital letters and punctuation:

Mr J. Hines	Mrs S. Lucas	Miss B. Smith	Ms T. Townsend
5 Sidney Rd	3 King Street	Balmy Holidays	24 Eastwood St
Wakefield	DN8 4QZ	London	NW4

4 Punctuate these addresses and write them in address form:

a miss f wood 3 brown street exworth essex e24 5sw
b mr 1 thompson 53 ashcroft rd edinburgh e5
c mr l price 8 saville street london w14
d mrs b stanton 23 heartshead st birmingham b15
e ms m grey denwood holidays 8 chester st glasgow g3

5 Formal letter layout

Read the letter and answer these questions:

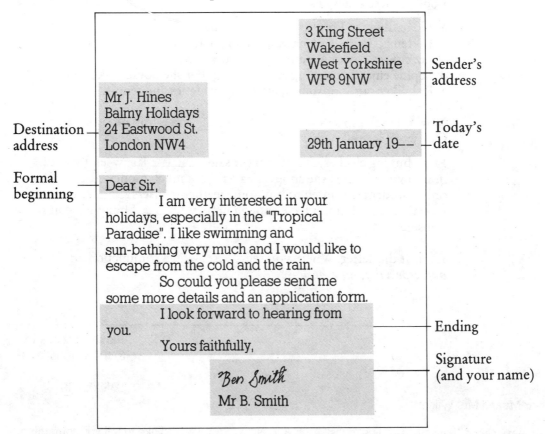

Sender's address
3 King Street
Wakefield
West Yorkshire
WF8 9NW

Destination address
Mr J. Hines
Balmy Holidays
24 Eastwood St.
London NW4

Today's date
29th January 19––

Formal beginning
Dear Sir,
   I am very interested in your holidays, especially in the "Tropical Paradise". I like swimming and sun-bathing very much and I would like to escape from the cold and the rain.
   So could you please send me some more details and an application form.
   I look forward to hearing from you.

Ending
   Yours faithfully,

Signature (and your name)
Ben Smith
Mr B. Smith

a Who is the letter from?
b Who is it to?
c What does Ben Smith want?

d **i** Beginning –
if you do not know the name of the person you are writing to:
    Dear Sir,
or Dear Sir or Madam,
or Dear Sirs,
or Dear Madam, (if you think the person you are writing to is a woman).

Ending: Yours faithfully,

ii Beginning –
if you know the name of the person you are writing to:
    Dear Mrs Jones,   *or* Dear Ms Trip,
or Dear Mr Hines,   *or* Dear Miss Jacobs,

Ending: Yours sincerely,

NOTES
Study the layout above and read these notes **a** to **e**:

a Your address:
At the top, on the right. Do not write your name.

b Destination address:
Below your address, on the left.

c The date:
    29th January 19––   *or* 29 January 19––
or January 29th 19––   *or* 29/1/19––
(In the U.S.A. the month goes before the day: 1/29/19––)

e Signature –
It can be difficult to read, so write your name clearly underneath it.

B Conjunctions

1 Look at these examples:

    a I love films, *so* I often go to the cinema.
    b I often go to the cinema *because* I love films.
    c Liz enjoys cooking, painting *and* travelling.
    d Sophie enjoys travelling and painting, *but* she doesn't like cooking.
    e Rob likes outdoor sports, *especially* athletics and tennis.

2 Now fill in the spaces with 'so', 'because', 'and', 'but' or 'especially'. One word is used twice.

I love buying clothes, _____ in the sales, _____ last week I went into town to look at the shops. I haven't got much money _____ I'm only a student. I wanted to buy some leather trousers _____ a jacket, _____ I didn't have enough money _____ I bought a pair of jeans instead.

3 Look at this letter. Where you see _____ add a conjunction *and, but, especially, so* or *because.*

Via della Scava 15
37100 Verona

12th May 19––

Dear Mr and Mrs Wilcox,

I am very happy that you can come to visit us in August _____ I would like to tell you something about my town.

The weather here in August is usually very good, _____ bring a warm jumper or jacket with you _____ it is sometimes cool in the evenings.

I know that you like going to the theatre _____ to the opera, _____ I have booked tickets for the performance of 'Aida' on 4th August. The opera starts at 9.00 in the evening. _____ there are a lot of people _____ the seats do not have numbers we must arrive very early.

I know that you will like the monuments in Verona, _____ the Arena and the Roman theatre.

There are a lot of good restaurants _____ cafés in Verona _____ we can try some of the local dishes. I am sure you will like our food, _____ the pasta dishes _____ the fruit ice-cream.

Please write to me soon _____ tell me what time you are arriving in Verona.

With best wishes,

Antonia Gelli

C Writing a formal letter

1 Work in pairs. Write out one letter each, change books and then check your partner's work.

I am looking forward to hearing from you.

3 Brown Street
Exworth
Essex E24 54W

so could you please send me an application form for the season ticket that you provide.

I love classical music, especially Mozart and Haydn, and I am very interested in your programme this year. I would like to see as many productions as possible,

16th April 19--

Yours faithfully,

so could you please send me a catalogue with more details and an order form.

I am very interested in your fashions, especially the winter dresses section,

10 Birch Grove
Retford
Notts.
DN33 WB1

October 8th 19--

I look forward to hearing from you.

Yours sincerely,

The Box Office
The Royal Opera House
Coventry Street
Liverpool
Merseyside L28

Dear Sir or Madam,

Mr L. Price
Elegant Fashions
53 Ashcroft St.
London W14

Dear Mr Price,

2 Here are the beginnings of three formal letters. They each ask for something:

---

16 The Avenue
Staines
Middlesex

Scottish Tourist Board
1 Waverley Street
Edinburgh

16th March 19—

Dear Sir or Madam,

---

247 Station Road
St Albans
Herts.
AL3 5DG

Hotel Dolomiten
Samnaun
Switzerland

22nd December 19—

Dear Sir or Madam,

42A Sydney St.
London N8

Box Office
Palace Theatre
Strand Street
London WC1

19th January 19—

Dear Sirs,

Here are the three letters, but they have been mixed up. Write out the letters in full.

I am writing to	ask about the tours
I would like to	confirm my telephone booking
I am writing to	confirm my reservation for

for two single rooms with bathroom	in August 19––.
three tickets for the performance of 'Othello'	from 9th to 15th March 19––.
of the Scottish lochs and Highlands	on Saturday 8th March.

Would you please	at the hotel on Sunday afternoon
We hope to arrive	in Edinburgh for the first
My husband and I will be	also send me two £7 tickets for 'Cats'

three weeks in August.	I enclose a postal order for £35 (5 × £7)
on 17th March.	I enclose a cheque for the deposit of £50.
at about 5.00.	I enclose a s.a.e.* for your reply.

Would you please send me	some information
Would you please also send me	a receipt
Would you please send me	the tickets

to the above address.	I look forward to hearing from you.
about the Edinburgh festival.	I look forward to hearing from you.
for the £50.00.	I look forward to hearing from you.

| Yours faithfully, |
| Yours faithfully, |
| Yours faithfully, |

* s.a.e. = stamped addressed envelope

3 Write your own letter.

Write a letter in reply to this advertisement asking for more information and an application form.

ENGLISH IN THE SUN

Do you like English?
Come to our summer holiday courses. Stay with an English family and have lessons every day with experienced teachers. Lots of excursions are organised to London, Oxford and Cambridge.

The school is in sunny Brighton on the south coast. For details and an application form, contact Ms R. Steele, Beachwater School, 3 Waterside Crescent, Brighton, BN4 3LY, England.

A Describing places

1 Anne Marshall and her childhood friend Tony went on holiday to the Rocky Hotel in Pandora. The advertisement gives one description of the hotel but Anne tells a different story to her friend.

Underline the adjectives in the two texts. Discuss them with your teacher or use a dictionary to help you understand them.

ROCKY HOTEL

This beautiful little family hotel stands near the lovely Irenian sea (ten minutes' walk from the hotel) with incredible views from every bedroom.

Enjoy delicious food prepared by the family or eat at interesting restaurants in the town centre (five minutes' walk from the hotel). Excellent fish dishes are a speciality of the area.

The night-life in Pandora is great, offering wonderful night-clubs or discotheques where you can dance all night. Have a fantastic time.

Rocky Hotel
11 Kings Parade
Pandora
9th June 19__

Dear Cathy,

Well, we arrived yesterday in Pandora, at the "beautiful little family hotel", remember the advert?

But it isn't beautiful, it's horrible – a horrible little house with a local family with two boring children on the ground floor.

The Irenian Sea is an hour away from the hotel and it is dirty. You can't see it from the windows and the views are awful – our view is the wall of the house next door!

The food is greasy and disgusting, and the portions are very small. Last night we went to a restaurant but it was expensive and the food was terrible there too.

Pandora is an interesting town, but the evenings are quiet – there's nothing to do... We are thinking of moving to the Balmy Holiday Club, by the sea.

2 Find eleven adjectives from the grid below. They are used in the advert and the letter on page 24. You can only read words across or down, not diagonally. This first one is done for you:

I	V	D	I	S	G	U	S	T	I	N	G	T	J
N	A	A	V	X	Z	O	Y	W	E	Q	Z	Q	A
T	E	R	R	I	B	L	E	T	Y	S	T	S	N
E	R	S	X	N	D	J	A	N	G	R	E	A	T
R	E	I	O	C	A	E	J	G	R	B	C	F	Y
E	K	H	O	R	R	I	B	L	E	Q	T	F	R
S	M	E	I	E	O	F	B	Z	A	V	N	A	P
T	P	V	F	D	B	I	L	D	S	Z	C	N	P
I	M	H	J	I	D	H	Q	Y	Y	T	A	T	T
N	A	W	C	B	D	B	U	W	A	A	I	A	D
G	T	Y	R	L	K	J	I	X	F	D	Z	S	N
T	I	C	O	E	X	C	E	L	L	E	N	T	R
E	N	F	G	Z	D	Z	T	L	B	K	L	I	N
I	A	W	F	U	L	S	X	Q	N	G	N	C	R

3 Now complete the text using adjectives from the grid:

Pandora is an _____ town situated on the north coast of Bahamia near the lovely Irenian Sea. The advertisement says that you can have a _____ time in Pandora, because the night-life is _____. It says that there are _____ views from the hotel and that the fish in the restaurants is _____.
Anne doesn't agree. She says the views from the hotel are _____ and the hotel is a _____ little house. She thinks the food is _____ and _____ in the hotel and _____ in the restaurant. She says that the evenings are very _____.

B Combining adjectives

1 Look at these sentences:

Bahamia has beautiful sandy beaches.
In Bahamia the beaches are beautiful and sandy.
Discuss the differences with your teacher.

2 Now complete the sentences below with 'and' only
where this is necessary, like this:

She has got long _____ dark hair.
Her hair is long __and__ dark.

  a The hotel is small _____ dirty.
  b Last night we went to a beautiful _____ little night-club.
  c We stayed in a quiet _____ friendly town called Pandora.
  d York Town is a large _____ industrial town.
  e The port, Bridlingpool, is noisy _____ exciting.
  f Come to exciting _____ historic London.
  g Leeds is a large _____ interesting city.
  h Yesterday we had a horrible _____ expensive meal.
  i My room in the hotel is small _____ dark.
  j The wonderful _____ little hotel is near the lovely _____ blue
Irenian Sea.

NOTE: Exception!! – *I have a black and white TV.*
When two colours come together they are joined by the word 'and'.
This is true if they come before or after the noun.

3 Write an advertisement for a place you know using some of the
adjectives you have learnt. Look at the advert on page 24 to help
you. Begin like this: *Come to . . .*

C Compound words

1 Look at the three phrases below. What do you think they mean?
Choose i or ii

  a a family hotel   i    or ii

  b a tennis ball   i   or ii

c a ham sandwich   i    or   ii

So which word names the object? The first word or the second word?
And which word is a noun used as an adjective?

2 Now look at these definitions and match them with the correct
phrase. The first one is done for you.

a a man who washes your windows	a wine-glass
b a place where you can dance, drink and meet people at night	a window cleaner
c a person who can mend your bicycle	a record player
d a machine that plays records	a coffee cup
e a cup which you use when you drink coffee	a night-club
f a glass which you use when you drink wine	a bicycle mechanic

3 **Activity**

Look at this example:

LIST ONE	LIST TWO
tennis	sandwich
ham	ball

You can make the compound words 'tennis ball' and 'ham
sandwich' from these lists.
Now make as many words as you can from the two lists. Use an
English/English dictionary to help you if you do not understand
individual words. Sometimes you can use one word twice.

LIST ONE		LIST TWO	
air	tennis	timetable	bill
beach	train	paper	shop
vegetable	bus	account	agency
brandy	shop	garden	glass
tea	wall	recorder	ball
mathematics	war	court	cup
family	bank	collar	party
travel	business	station	doctor
cassette	gas	film	teacher
garden	shirt	trip	camp
holiday	clothes	window	hostess

Now write six sentences using the words you have learnt.

D Weather

1 Match the pictures with the correct descriptions:

2 Look at the difference between these two sentences and discuss:

a 'Oh no! It's raining and I haven't got my umbrella!'
b It often rains in Bolton in August.

Can you say when we write 'It's raining' and when we write 'It rains'?

In **a** we are describing something that is happening now (at the moment of speaking), and in **b** we are describing something that happens regularly (often, in this case).

i Choose **a** or **b** to complete these sentences:

1 Please be quiet. I **a** work.
                     b am working.

2 Anne **a** goes   to Bahamia for her holidays every year.
        b is going

3 She **a** stays   at the Balmy Holiday Club every summer.
       b is staying

4 Now she **a** sunbathes   on the beach.
           b is sunbathing

5 Her friend Tony **a** works   in the kitchen at the moment.
                   b is working

6 Many people **a** play   tennis in the summer.
               b are playing

7 Where's Richard? He **a** goes   to London.
                       b is going

8 What is Richard doing? He **a** reads   the newspaper.
                             b is reading

9 The train **a** leaves   at 5.30 every day.
             b is leaving

10 At the moment Richard's friend **a** waits   for him at the
                                   b is waiting
station in London.

ii Below are two texts. One is a description of the climate in Scotland
and the other is an extract from the weather forecast for today in
Edinburgh. Each line belongs to one text. The lines are mixed up.
Work in pairs. One student should write the text about weather, the
other student about climate. Read each other's text for mistakes.

  1 In Scotland the climate is moderate, and the weather
  2 '... and now for the weather. Today in Edinburgh
  3 is very changeable. On the east coast
  4 temperatures are rising and
  5 it is often windy and it rains a lot, but in winter
  6 the sun is shining. It is a bit windy and
  7 it is sometimes foggy. There are often dry days when
  8 the sky is blue although it is usually cold.
  9 the sky is blue at the moment, but clouds
10 are coming in from the west.

11 In summer it is often humid and the sun shines
12 sometimes, but it rains a lot and the temperature
13 We can expect some rain for this afternoon, so get
14 your umbrellas out . . .
15 doesn't often rise above 25°C.

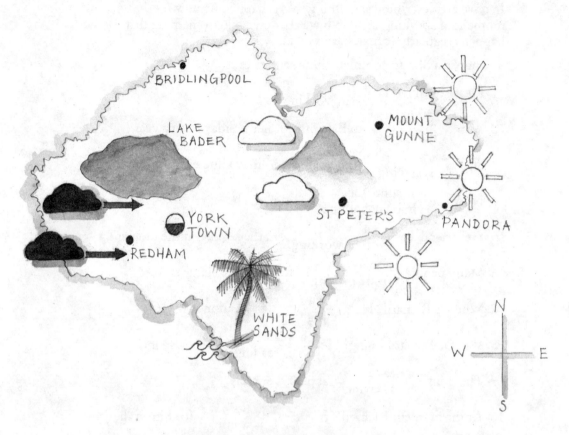

3 Look at the weather map for Bahamia today and write a weather forecast. Look at the text about Edinburgh for help.

Key

☀ — SUN

☁ CLOUDS — AND RAIN

☁ — CLOUDY

Begin like this:
Today on the east coast . . .

E Postcards

1 Postcard One

> 1 Dear Jennie,
>
> How are you?
>
> 2 Having a good time. Weather's not bad but Pandora's a bit boring.
>
> 3 Enjoying a drink in the hotel bar at the moment – Anne's having a shower.
>
> 4 Went to White Sands Beach for a swim yesterday and hired mopeds then went to Lake Bader – very pretty.
>
> 5 Thinking of leaving Pandora – we'd like to get a job in the Balmy Holiday Club by the sea – cos we haven't got much money left.
>
> Hope to see you soon.
>
> Tony and Anne

Mrs Jennie Field
753 High Street,
Bradford,
Yorkshire
BD1 7GD,
ENGLAND.

NOTE: 'cos' = 'because'. This is a very informal short form.

Read the postcard and answer the questions:

a Who wrote the postcard? (Read it carefully and think about the answer.)
b Do Tony and Anne like Pandora? Why?
c Where is Anne?
d How many places did they visit yesterday?
e Where do they want to work? Why?

2 Now look again at the postcard and put the number of the sections in the boxes below. The first one is done for you:

A Past activities.   `4`
B Description of weather and place.
C Plans for the future.
D What the writer is doing at the moment.
E Greetings.

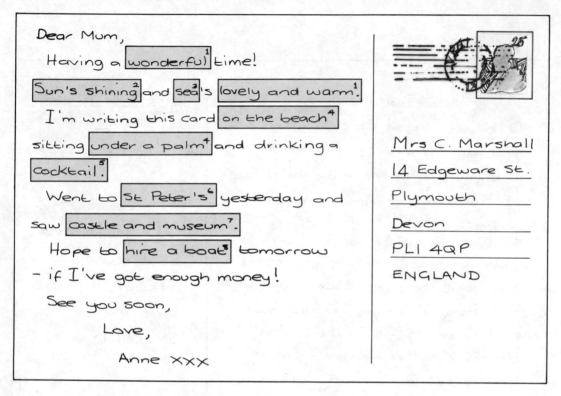

Dear Mum,

Having a |wonderful|¹ time!

|Sun's shining|² and |sea|³'s |lovely and warm|¹.

I'm writing this card |on the beach|⁴ sitting |under a palm|⁴ and drinking a |cocktail|⁵.

Went to |St Peter's|⁶ yesterday and saw |castle and museum|⁷.

Hope to |hire a boat|⁸ tomorrow - if I've got enough money!

See you soon,

Love,

Anne xxx

Mrs C. Marshall
14 Edgeware St.
Plymouth
Devon
PL1 4QP
ENGLAND

NOTE XXX = kisses

Use this postcard as a model to write one of your own. The list below gives you different expressions to put in the boxes.

e.g. Box 1: *Having a* |*wonderful¹*| *time.*
could change to
Having a horrible time.

Be careful to make all the right changes to verbs and articles.

Now imagine you are on holiday in one of the places below and write your postcard.

A beach in England	Swiss Mountains
A historical city	The Mysterious Orient
A Greek island	The U.S.A.

1 fantastic, lovely, interesting, exciting, incredible, horrible, awful.
2 it's cold/hot, it's raining/snowing, it's foggy/windy/cloudy.
3 the mountains, the beach, the town, the countryside.
4 in a bar/café, outside the cathedral, on top of a mountain, in the museum, in the shopping centre.
5 coffee, tea, coca-cola (coke), beer, glass of wine, milkshake.
6 Barcelona, Honolulu, Montreal, Chartres.
7 theatre, park, zoo, museum, cathedral, church.
8 rent a car, go on a boat-trip, do some water-skiing, hire a wind-surf, go for a ride in a helicopter.

4 Look at the sentences below and discuss them with your teacher:

(I'm) having a wonderful time!
(The) hotel is awful.
(I/We) changed hotels yesterday.

Now write these sentences in their expanded forms. The first is done for you.

a Having a good time.   *I'm having a good time.*
b Weather's not bad.
c Having a drink in the hotel bar.
d Went to White Sands beach.
e Hired mopeds.
f Thinking of leaving Pandora.
g cos it's too hot
  (see NOTE on Postcard One)
h Hope to see you soon.

5 Now look at these sentences and write the shorter forms. The first is done for you.

a I wish you were here!   *Wish you were here!*
b I'm staying at a lovely hotel.
c The beach is long and sandy.
d I hope to see John tomorrow.
e because
f I ate in a fantastic restaurant yesterday.
g It's raining heavily.
h I'll speak to you soon.

6 Now go out and buy a postcard and write in English to a friend or your parents.

UNIT 5

A Places

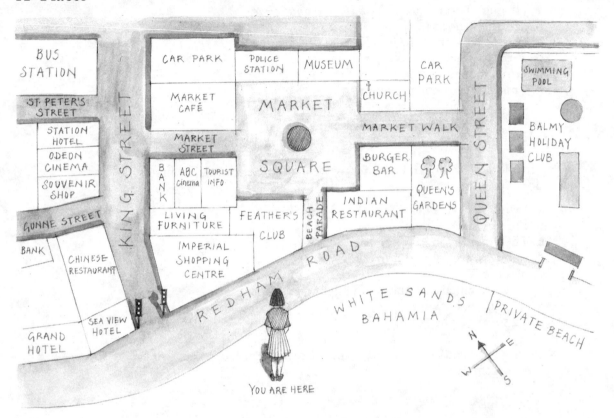

1 Look at the map of White Sands. Do you understand what all the places are? If not, look them up in your dictionary or ask your teacher.

2 i Look at these prepositions:

   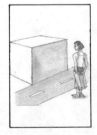 

on the corner of King Street and West Road

between

on the left of **on the right of**

opposite

Mary is **next to** Tom. Fred is **next to** Tom Jack is **near** Mary

ii Look at the map of White Sands again, and then write out these sentences with the correct preposition (in some cases there is more than one possibility). Compare your answers with another student and discuss any differences.

a Seaview Hotel is _____ the Chinese Restaurant and _____ the Imperial Shopping Centre. It is _____ King Street and Redham Road.

b The Station Hotel is _____ the Market Café, and _____ the Odeon cinema. It is _____ King Street and St Peter's Street.

c The Odeon cinema is _____ the Station Hotel and the souvenir shop.

d The King Street bank is _____ the ABC cinema and _____ the souvenir shop.

e The Indian restaurant is _____ Queen's Gardens.

f The Queen Street car park is _____ the church and _____ the Balmy Holiday Club.

g The Police Station is _____ the museum and _____ the Feathers Club.

h The Imperial Shopping Centre is _____ King Street and Beach Parade _____ the beach. It is _____ the traffic lights on King Street.

i The Feathers Club is _____ Imperial Shopping Centre.

j The bus station is _____ the King Street car park.

k The ABC cinema is _____ the bank and the tourist information office. It is _____ the Market Café.

l The Imperial Shopping Centre is _____ King Street and Redham Road.

3 Look at the map of the Balmy Holiday Club, and write where the places are:

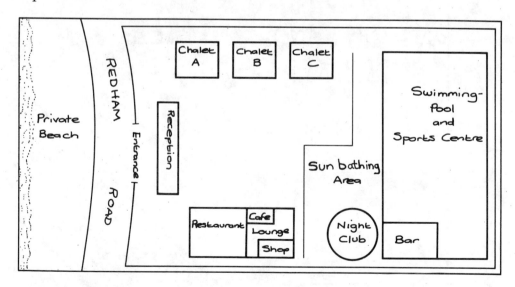

Begin like this:
At the Balmy Holiday Club, the entrance is opposite the private beach. The restaurant is _____

4 a Look at the map of White Sands. Choose a street in White Sands. You are in this street. Write a short description of the things near you. Do not use the name of the street.

b Work in pairs. Read your text to your partner. Stop when he/she knows which street you are in. Now listen to his/her description and say which street he/she is in.

c Now write a description of where your partner is.

d Now compare your descriptions. How are they different?

B Informal invitations and suggestions

1 Look at the poster and answer the questions:

  a What kind of food can you buy at the barbecue?
  b What is the price for people who belong to the club?
  c What is the price for people who do not belong to the club?
  d What is the date of the barbecue?
  e What time does the barbecue start?
  f What can you do at the barbecue?

2 Now we are going to learn how to write and reply to informal invitations, between friends or people who know each other well.

Anne Marshall and Tony Field are working at the Balmy Holiday Club. Look at the NOTES below where you will see alternatives to the numbered sentences.

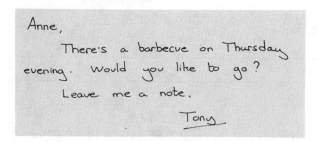

Anne,

There's a barbecue on Thursday evening. Would you like to go?

Leave me a note.

Tony

Now look at her reply:

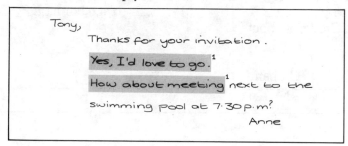

Tony,

Thanks for your invitation.

Yes, I'd love to go.[1]

How about meeting[1] next to the swimming pool at 7.30 p.m?

Anne

NOTES

1 Ways of accepting an invitation (Alternatives)

Yes, I'd love to + VERB
Yes, that's a great idea.
Yes, I'd like to.

Ways of refusing an invitation

I'm sorry I can't come because ... (REASON)
I'm afraid I can't come because ... (REASON)
(REASON: I'm going to the theatre/I'm very busy at the moment/
I promised to meet my friend, etc.)

2 Ways of suggesting

How about + VERB + —ing?   e.g.: How about meeting at six?
Let's + VERB   e.g.: Let's go to the cinema.
Why don't we + VERB?   e.g.: Why don't we go home?
Shall we + VERB?   e.g.: Shall we have a drink?

3 Look at these invitation letters and the replies:

Dear Sue,
There's a barbecue on Thursday. (1) _____.
Love,
Anne.

Dear Anne,
I'm sorry (2) _____.
I'm going to the cinema.
Love,
Sue

Dear Don,
(3) _____ to the football match on Saturday? (4) _____ spending the day in London?
Mike

Dear Mike,
Thanks for your note. Yes, (5) _____.
(6) _____ go in Jack's minibus. It would save a lot of money.
Cheers!
Don

Dear Fiona,
I've got two free tickets for the opera on Friday. (7) _____ _____ come with me? It starts at 8.30, so (8) _____ _____ in the Crown at about 7.30?
Love,
Graham

Dear Graham,
Thank you for your invitation to the opera. (9) _____ busy on Friday.
(10) _____ go another night?
F.

Put the correct number in the box next to the correct expression. The first one is done for you.

Let's	6	How about	☐
Would you like to	☐	Why don't we	☐
shall we meet	☐	Would you like to go	☐
I'm afraid I'm	☐	I'd like to	☐
Would you like to go?	☐	I can't because	☐

4 Writing an invitation

Imagine this is your diary for next week:

Copy it out into your exercise book – make sure it is big enough for you to fill in.

Now complete the diary for three different evenings. Use this table to help you:

PLACE	TIME	MEETING PLACE
Cinema	8 p.m.	Café
Disco	9.15 p.m.	Bus stop
Pop concert	7.30 p.m.	Your house
Restaurant	10 p.m.	Your office

Here is an example:

Monday	Cinema 10 p.m.	meet at bus stop

Now write a note to three other students inviting them to go out with you. Choose from this table:

PLACE	TIME	MEETING PLACE
Party	7.30 p.m.	Your house
Theatre	8.15 p.m.	Underground station
Pub	10 p.m.	Outside the Grand Hotel
Football match	11 p.m.	Pub – "The Sun"
Nightclub	8.30 p.m.	Outside your school

You can choose any day but you should suggest a time and a place to meet.

Now give your notes to the students you are inviting. When *you* receive an invitation, look at your diary and write a reply, saying either YES or NO. Use the examples on pages 37 and 38 to help you.

5 Invitation consequences

Take a big piece of paper. Think of two people, a man and a woman (famous people, or students in the class). Think of a place where they meet. He invites her to do something and she replies. Think where they go and what happens.

At the top of a piece of paper, write the man's name and the word 'met'. Fold the paper over and pass it to the student on your right. Take the paper from the student on your left and write the woman's name on this new piece of paper. Fold it again, pass it to the right and continue. Fold the paper each time after you write on it.

1 FOLD →	(Male name) met
2 FOLD →	(Female name)
3 FOLD →	At/in (a place)
4 FOLD →	He said ' ' (an invitation)
5 FOLD →	She replied ' '
6 FOLD →	So they went to (a place)
	And (the result of the story)

When you have finished unfold the piece of paper and read out your stories. They can be very funny!

C Paragraphs

1 Read the letter and answer the questions:

LETTER A

3 St Peter's Street
White Sands
Bahamia SW4 3V5
26th July 19--

Dear Anne,

How are you? I have a bad cold and the doctor says I must stay at home for two days, so I'm staying in bed and taking aspirin every four hours. How was the barbecue? I'm sorry I couldn't come. Was the food ok? The weather wasn't very good, was it? Anyway, I went to the cinema with John. We saw 'Time for Tea' with Tina Taylor. The story was awful but the photography was lovely- lots of scenes of the English countryside in spring. After the film we went for a walk in the rain, and that's why I've got this cold. Would you like to come for dinner next Friday? I'm going to invite Helen and Tim as well, and I want to try out a new Italian recipe. Hope to see you then - about 8.00?

Love,

Sue

a Why is Sue taking aspirins?
b Did she go to the barbecue?
c What film did she see?
d Did she like the film?
e What kind of food is Sue going to cook on Friday?

2 Now look at Letter B. What is the difference between Letters A and
B? Discuss with your teacher.

LETTER B

> 3 St Peter's Street
> White Sands
> Bahamia SW4 3V5
> 29th July 19--
>
> Dear Anne,
>
> How are you? I have a bad cold and the
> doctor says I must stay at home for two days, so
> I'm staying in bed and taking aspirin every four
> hours. — Writer's health
>
> How was the barbecue? I'm sorry I
> couldn't come. Was the food ok? The weather wasn't
> very good, was it? — Barbecue
>
> Anyway, I went to the cinema with
> John. We saw 'Time for Tea' with Tina Taylor.
> The story was awful but the photography was
> lovely — lots of scenes of the English countryside
> in spring. After the film we went for a walk in
> the rain, and that's why I've got this cold. — Cinema and John
>
> Would you like to come for dinner
> next Friday? I'm going to invite Helen and
> Tim as well, and I want to try out a new
> Italian recipe. Hope to see you then —
> about 8.00? — Invitation to dinner
>
> Love,
>
> Sue

3 Look at the 'titles' at the side of each paragraph in Letter B. Now look at this text and invent titles for each paragraph. Write your titles in the spaces next to the paragraphs.

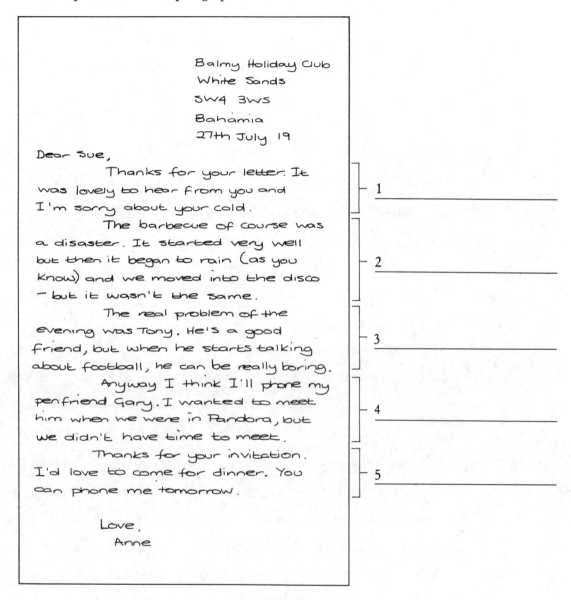

Balmy Holiday Club
White Sands
SW4 3WS
Bahamia
27th July 19

Dear Sue,

Thanks for your letter. It was lovely to hear from you and I'm sorry about your cold.

1 _____

The barbecue of course was a disaster. It started very well but then it began to rain (as you know) and we moved into the disco – but it wasn't the same.

2 _____

The real problem of the evening was Tony. He's a good friend, but when he starts talking about football, he can be really boring.

3 _____

Anyway I think I'll phone my penfriend Gary. I wanted to meet him when we were in Pandora, but we didn't have time to meet.

4 _____

Thanks for your invitation. I'd love to come for dinner. You can phone me tomorrow.

5 _____

Love,
Anne

4 Work with a partner. Imagine that you want to write a description (not a letter) of White Sands, or a town you know. You want to write five paragraphs. Write down the 'titles' for the five paragraphs in the order you think is best. Do not show them to your partner.

Now take a new piece of paper and write the description, using the paragraph titles. Set it out like Letter B, page 42, leaving spaces next to the different paragraphs. When you have finished, change papers with your partner and write titles for his/her paragraphs. Now compare them to the original titles.

5 Look at Tony's letter. What is incorrect about the way it is written?

Balmy Holiday Club,
Redham Road,
White Sands,
Bahamia
20th July 19--

Dear Richard,

How are you? I hope you're well. Anne and I stayed in Pandora for one terrible week. The hotel was disgusting and the town was very expensive. Then we came to White Sands on an excursion and we found the Balmy Holiday Club. We both like the island and we wanted to stay here, so we asked if they had any jobs, and they said they had and took us on* as summer assistants. So now everything is fine, and we love it here. The club has a lot of things to do. There's a sports centre, a swimming pool and a private beach. It is in a lovely position opposite some gardens, and next to the sea, of course. All the food and accommodation is free because we're working here. It's great! White Sands is a holiday town really, but there is everything you need in the centre. The town is built round a square where there is a very interesting museum and a really good night-club - the Feathers Club. There are some good places to eat - a Burger bar, a café and an Indian restaurant. There are no trains on the island, but there's a bus station in King Street. Anyway, I'm really writing because I know you are looking for a job - and I think there are some jobs still available here, so why don't you write and ask?

Regards,

Tony

* take someone on = give someone a job

Look at the paragraph titles below, and put them in the correct order by number according to Tony's letter. Write the numbers in the boxes provided.

a Suggestion to write and ask about a job.
b How Tony and Anne found Balmy Holidays and jobs.
c Pandora – a great disappointment.
d Description of the club.
e Description of the town.

Now mark the beginning and end of the paragraphs on the letter like this:

_____.// _____.//

    e.g.: *Dear Richard,*
            //How are you?

6 Write a letter to a pen-friend, inviting her/him to come to your town. Write a list of paragraph titles first to help you organise your letter.

A Instructions

Balmy Holiday Club

1 Breakfast is from 8 a.m.–9 a.m.
  Lunch is from 1 p.m.–2 p.m.
  Dinner is from 8 p.m.–9.30 p.m.
2 Please do not take food or drink into your rooms.
3 Please be quiet after 11.30 p.m.
4 Please tidy your rooms every morning.
5 If you have any problems, contact our assistant at Reception.
6 For information about special activities and excursions, please contact Miss Smith at Reception.
7 Please do not smoke in your rooms.
8 Please leave your rooms by 11 a.m. on the last day of your holiday.

Have a good time and come back next year!

1 Look at the regulations for the 'Balmy Holiday Club'. Answer these questions *True* (T) or *False* (F); **a** is done for you.

a You can have dinner at 9.00 p.m. ⊤
b You can have breakfast at 8.30 a.m. ☐
c You can have a party in your room at midnight. ☐
d You can find help at Reception. ☐
e You can go on special excursions. ☐
f You can smoke in your rooms. ☐
g On your last day, you can stay in your room until midday. ☐

2 Look at these examples:

a Please **tidy** your rooms every morning.
b Please **do not take** food or drink into your rooms.

Both these sentences give instructions. **a** is a positive and **b** a negative instruction.

Look again at the Balmy Holiday Club instructions on page 46 and underline all the verbs which give instructions, like this:

Please <u>tidy</u> your rooms every morning.

What do you think the grammatical rules are for giving instructions? Discuss with your teacher.

3 Susan Peterson is 17 and she goes to a private school. She wrote to her Spanish pen-friend Elena telling her about the school. This is part of the letter:

> ..... Now I'm in the sixth form it's much better at school. We have our own house, separate from the rest of the school, where we can go and study or relax, and there are kitchens where we can cook lunch too, if we want to.
> There are still a lot of rules, of course. We can only cook lunch between 12.00 and 1.30 p.m., and we must wash up immediately after lunch. We can't smoke in the house, and we must be quiet during the day because some of the rooms are used for lessons. There is a small library, but we can't take the books home, and we've even got a stereo cassette recorder, but we mustn't play it during lesson times. And, of course, when we go home, we have to lock the door!
> So you see, there are rules, but it's a lot better than last year ...

Look at the text above and write out the house rules, using 'instruction language' like this:

> Please cook between 12.00 and 1.30 p.m. only.

Find five rules!

4 **Quiz**

In this quiz, work in pairs. Listen to your teacher's example. Then think of a similar situation or place.

Write *at least* five instructions for the situation.
e.g. Situation – You are in a library.

Instructions – Do not speak loudly.
Do not smoke.
Do not eat or drink.
Ask the assistant for help.
Fill in a card if you want to take out a book.

Now students read out their instructions and guess each other's situations.

B Directions

When you write directions, you usually give them more precisely than when speaking. Giving landmarks is very helpful. For example, in Britain, people often use pubs to give directions: 'Turn left at the "Rose and Crown", then go straight on until you see the "Black Bull", then turn left ...' etc.

1 Look at these examples:

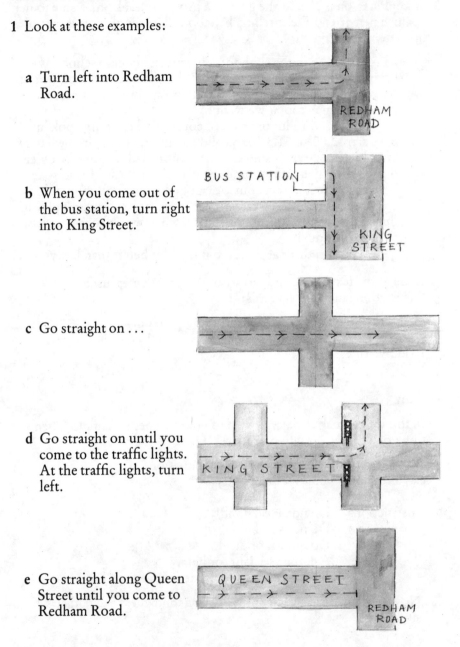

a Turn left into Redham Road.

b When you come out of the bus station, turn right into King Street.

c Go straight on ...

d Go straight on until you come to the traffic lights. At the traffic lights, turn left.

e Go straight along Queen Street until you come to Redham Road.

Discuss the difference between 'Go straight on' and 'Go straight along Redham Road' with your teacher.

2 Look at the map below. Then read Anne's letter to Gary and draw the two routes she describes on the map. Like this:

The car route is started for you.

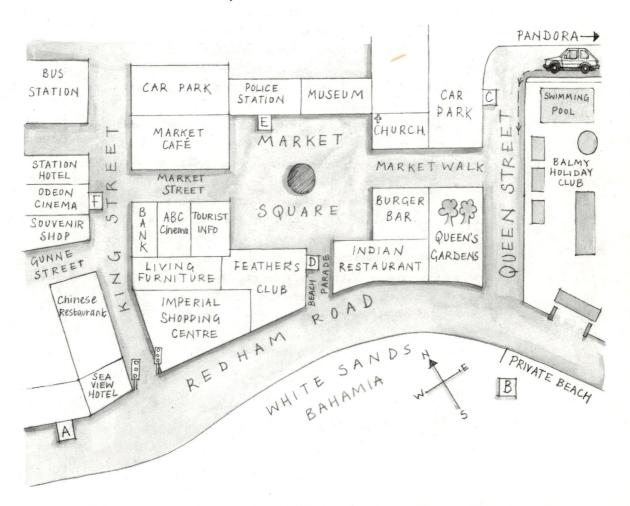

This is part of the letter Anne wrote to Gary, inviting him to the Balmy Holiday Club:

... The club is very easy to find. If you come by car you take the main road from Pandora to White Sands. When you come into Queen Street, go straight on until you come to the sea. Turn left into Redham Road and the club is on the left.

If you come by bus, the White Sands bus takes you to the bus station in King Street and then you can walk. When you come out of the bus station, turn right, and go straight on until you come to the traffic lights. Then at the traffic lights turn left. Go straight along Redham Road past the Feathers Club and the Indian restaurant. The Balmy Holiday Club is on the left after Queen Street. When you arrive, the reception is opposite the entrance. Go there and ask for me. I'll come and meet you.

Hope to see you next week.

Love,

Anne

3 Look at the map on page 49. Then read the texts below. Each text directs someone to a different place (for example, the Odeon cinema). In each text write in the correct letter and the place. The first one is done for you. The directions are always from the bus station.

a When you come out of the bus station, turn right, then walk straight on until you come to the Odeon cinema on the right. At the cinema, turn left into Market Street. Go straight along Market Street, across Market Square, and along Market Walk until you come to Queen Street. Turn left into Queen Street, and I'll meet you there. The _car park_ is on the left. The letter is _C_.

b When you come out of the bus station, turn right, and walk along King Street until you come to the _____ on the right, opposite Market Street. I'll meet you there. The letter is _____.

c When you come out of the bus station, turn right, and go straight on until you come to the Odeon cinema on the right. Turn left opposite the cinema into Market Street. Walk straight along Market Street, and then turn left into Market Square. I'll meet you at the _____ between the market café and the museum. The letter is ____.

d When you come out of the bus station, turn right, and go straight along King Street until you come to the traffic lights. Turn left at the traffic lights into Redham Road. Go straight along Redham Road, past the Feathers Club and walk until you come to Queen Street on the left. I'll meet you at the _____ on the right opposite the Balmy Holiday Club entrance. The letter is ____.

e When you come out of the bus station turn right into King Street. Go straight on until you come to the traffic lights. Turn left at the traffic lights into Redham Road. Go straight on past the Imperial Shopping Centre on the left and turn left into Beach Parade. I'll meet you next to the _____ in Beach Parade on the left. The letter is ____.

f When you come out of the bus station, turn right into King Street. Go straight along King Street until you come to the traffic lights. Turn right at the traffic lights into Redham Road and I'll meet you outside the _____ opposite the sea. The letter is ____.

4 Now choose a place on the map. Write the directions for your friend to meet you there. Look at the texts above to help you. _Do not_ write the name of the place where you want to meet him/her. Leave a space _____. Then exchange books with another student and read the directions in his/her book. Follow them on the map, and write in the name of the place where you will meet. Compare your answers.

C Telephone messages

1

Anne,

    Gary phoned from
Pandora at 10.00 a.m.
He's arriving this evening-
about 7.30 p.m.
    Wait for him at
Reception.
       Tony

Answer these qustions:

a Who did Gary telephone?

b Who answered the telephone?

c What was the message?

2 Look at this model with your teacher:

Message is for this person — Anne,

Name of person who telephoned — Gary phoned from

Place he/she telephoned from — Pandora at 10.00 a.m. — Time of phone call

He's arriving this evening- about 7.30 p.m.

Message — Wait for him at Reception.

Tony — Name of person who took the message

Look at the language in this message. You will see that it is very simple and does not include unnecessary details. We do not always write complete sentences, and we often leave out words which are not very important when we write messages.

3 Read this telephone conversation.

Drrinngg ... drrinngg ...
Peter: Hello, Wakefield 36829.
Julie: Hello, Peter? This is Julie, Julie Martin.
Peter: Oh, hi, Julie, how are you?
Julie: Fine, thanks, what about you?
Peter: Not so bad. Did you want to speak to Elaine?
Julie: Yes, I did. Is she there?
Peter: No, I'm afraid she's out at the moment and I don't know
        when she'll be back. Can I take a message?
Julie: Yes ... I just wanted to say that I can't meet her this
        afternoon because I have to go to Leeds, but I can meet her
        tomorrow at 6.30 p.m. at Mantovani's for a drink if she wants.
Peter: Mantovani's ... 6.30 p.m. for a drink. OK, I'll leave a
        message. Is that everything?
Julie: Yes, I think so. Oh, you can tell her to phone me tomorrow
        morning at the office.
Peter: OK. Fine. Bye for now, then.
Julie: Bye.

Now write the message Peter left for Elaine. Use the models in **1** and
2 to help you.

4 Now work in pairs.

Sit back to back if possible.
Telephone your partner with a message for another student in your
class.
Listen to your partner's message.
Write his/her message on a piece of paper for the student he/she
wanted to contact. Use the model in **2** to help you.
Give him/her the message.

A Writing about the past

1 Read this extract from Anne's diary, then answer the questions:

Saturday ...... 6th.

Met Gary for the first time yesterday. He arrived while I was sunbathing. Wow! He's so good-looking! When he gave me the red roses I didn't know what to say.

Well, we went for a walk by the sea, then he took me to a romantic little restaurant where we ate fish and drank champagne. After dinner he said, 'Let's go to the Feathers Club' – so of course we went and we danced and talked until two. Before I went home he invited me to go out in his boat tomorrow and, of course, I said, 'Yes'.

Worked in the club all morning, prepared breakfast, washed up, tidied the bedrooms, made the beds, swept the floors etc. How I hate this job! Still, this afternoon I'm meeting Gary and we're going sailing. Life is so confusing. Last week I wanted to go back to England, but after meeting Gary I'm not so sure.

a Did Anne know Gary before Friday?
b Did Anne enjoy her evening with Gary?
c Does Anne enjoy her job?
d Where did she want to go last week?

2 Look at Anne's dairy again and find the past tense of these words. If you do not know the meanings, look them up in your dictionary. Make two lists, one of regular verbs with the past tense ending in '–ed', and one of irregular verbs:

wash	dance	make	arrive
meet	talk	eat	say
sweep	tidy	prepare	drink
give	want	invite	is

Example:

	REGULAR		IRREGULAR
	work worked		go went

B Ordering events

1 The two expressions in **a** and the two expressions in **b** mean the same thing.

Look at these examples:

a 1 After leaving school,   she went to university.
    2 After she left school,   she went to university.

This means: She left school (first), she went to university (second).

b 1 He closed all the windows   before leaving the house.
    2 He closed all the windows   before he left the house.

This means: He closed the windows (first), he left the house (second).

2 Now write two sentences for each of the pictures below. Use the past tense and either 'before' or 'after'. Choose the verbs you need from the list below. Check the past tense in the dictionary if you are not sure of the form. The first one is done for you:

He washed the car before going on holiday.

He washed the car before he went on holiday.

a

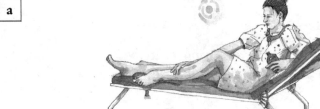 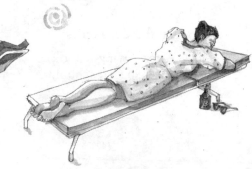

b

c

d

sunbathe   take off
buy   go
eat   put on
brush

C Description and action in the past

1 Look at this example:

He *arrived* while I *was sunbathing*.

One verb describes the general situation (what was happening at the time), the other describes a single action which continues the story. Which verb describes the situation and which describes the action? What is the difference? There are three similar sentences below. Find the two different types of verb and discuss them with your teacher.

a The phone rang while I was washing my hair.
b It started to rain while I was repairing the roof.
c My dog ran away while I was walking in the park.

2 Look at the text below. The verbs have been underlined. Decide which verbs describe the situation and put them in column one. Decide which verbs describe actions that continue the story and put them in column two. The first one is done for you.

It <u>was raining</u>. Peter <u>came</u> out of the pub and <u>lit</u> a cigarette. The shops <u>were closing</u>. He <u>walked</u> over to the bus stop. Some tourists <u>were playing</u> the guitar and others <u>were singing</u>. Peter <u>waited</u> for his bus.

Column One – Situations   Column Two – Actions that continue the story

a *was raining*   a
b   b
c   c
d   d

We call the verb form in column one the 'past continuous', and the form in column two the 'simple past'.

3 Look at this picture and describe the situation. Discuss it with your teacher.

1893 – Deadpalm Junction – Bahamia – A very dangerous town

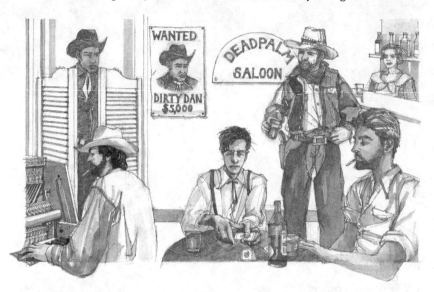

4 a Now write three sentences about the situation. Use the past continuous tense. Begin like this:

It was a quiet day in Deadpalm. A few people were sitting in the saloon...

b When suddenly! – Discuss what happened with your partner. (Who was standing outside the door, do you think?)
Now write three sentences about what happened. Use the simple past tense. Begin like this:
Suddenly the door opened ....

5 Compare what you wrote with the other students' stories. Is it different?

6 In the following text, choose the correct form of the verb. Cross out the *wrong* form of the verb.
e.g. *The day was fine and the sun ~~shone~~/was shining when we left home.*

Yesterday evening Steve went/was going to the Odeon cinema. When he arrived/was arriving, he saw/was seeing a few other people who talked/were talking outside the ticket office. While he waited/was waiting for his friend Pete, he looked/was looking at the other people in the queue. One woman was different from the others. She wore/was wearing an elegant black dress with a brown leather belt. He suddenly remembered/was remembering her face. He said/was saying, 'Marsha, do you remember me?' She replied/was replying, 'Oh, Steve, what a surprise! We last met/were meeting on the train to Cardiff, when the train broke/was breaking down, and we drank/were drinking coffee together for two hours.'

7 Often the simple past and the past continuous are combined when one action in a story interrupts another action which describes the general situation.
Look at this diagram:

```
            Gary arrived                        now
                 │                               │
─────────── T  I │ M  E ───────────────          ↓
          ◄───────────────────────►
            Anne was sunbathing
```

This situation can be expressed in two ways:

A – Anne was sunbathing *when* Gary arrived
B – Gary arrived *while* Anne was sunbathing

Look at these sentences and put in 'when' or 'while'.

a We were working _____ the door opened.
b I worked as a waiter _____ I was living in Hull.
c They came _____ she was writing a letter.
d They were playing tennis _____ it began to rain.
e I thought about my holiday _____ I was walking in the park.
f I was sitting in the garden _____ John told me the news.

8 In this exercise, use the pictures on the left to complete the sentences on the right.

a I was _____ for the bus when I _____ my friend Julia.

b Philip's mother _____ _____ he _____ _____ dinner.

c Joan was _____ _____ the telephone _____ .

d I _____ the accident _____ I _____ _____ _____ _____ street.

D Giving more information

1 Look at this sentence:

    Water is a transparent liquid.

  Let us imagine that we want to add more information:

    It boils at 100°C and freezes at 0°C.

  We can join these two sentences using 'which':

    Water is a transparent liquid which boils at 100°C and freezes at 0°C.

  If we want to give more information about a person, we use 'who':

    A postman is a man who delivers letters.

  When we write English we use:

WHO –
to give more information about *people*.

WHICH –
to give more information about *things*, *subjects*, and *places*.

WHERE –
a to give more information about a place:
    e.g. This is the part of Paris where I live.
b instead of a preposition (at, in, on etc.) + WHICH:
    e.g. This is the part of the film where he meets the girl.

2 Write out these sentences and put 'who', 'which', or 'where' in the space.
  a It is a little market _____ you can buy fruit.
  b My girl-friend, _____ works in advertising, has changed her job.
  c There is a new hairdresser's in the High Street _____ you can have your hair cut for only £5.50.
  d Growles's last book, _____ was published in 1956, was a big success.
  e Nobody noticed the Russian agents _____ were watching Baxter carefully.
  f Suddenly he saw the car _____ he had parked in the High Street.
  g They walked down to the village _____ was in a small valley.
  h We went to the village pub _____ we met George Riley and his friends.
  i He was a man _____ wanted too much.
  j St Alfred's Station, _____ was designed by Sir Gladstone Walsh, was completed in 1864.

3 The following piece has a number of phrases missing. Fill in the spaces from the list below using the relevant letter. Some of the answers are interchangeable.

  My cousin Walter, (1) _____, is a very strange character. First, his left eye, (2) _____, is different from his right eye, (3) _____.

Second, he never eats: he only drinks, and he drinks a kind of beer, a thick black beer, (4) _____. Third, he has a large piano in his kitchen, (5) _____. Finally, in the garden, (6) _____, Walter has a sofa and three armchairs. And the TV? Walter keeps the TV in the garage, (7) _____.

a which he plays during the night
b where he can watch it while sitting in his car
c which is blue
d where most people have flowers and plants
e who is ten years older than me
f which is green
g which he keeps in his sitting room

E Sending a telex

1 Look at these abbreviations, often used in telexes:

ATTN – Attention – this telex is for the attention of . . .
EEEEE – Error – the last word or words are not correct
TLX or TX – Telex
PLS – Please
ASAP – As soon as possible
TKS – Thanks
RGDS – Regards
RCVD YR TLX – Received your telex
STG/LSTG – £ sterling (pounds sterling)
TRNSFR – Transfer
INCL – Including
ACCM – Accommodation
NO – Number

NOTE: If you receive or write telexes regularly, you will learn the abbreviations which are used in your business. Do not invent these – wait until you have seen them in a telex you have received before using them.

2 Now look at these descriptions of telexes which were received or sent by a language school in Pandora. Match them with the telexes on the next pages:

a A travel agent would like to book a language course for a student.
b The language school accepts the travel agent's booking.
c A man would like information about a course for his son.
d An urgent request for a reply to another telex.
e A telex giving the boy's father information about a course.
f A telex confirming that some money will be sent to the school.

1

298574 STARLET 2
5839477PANDORA P
5 APRIL 1986
05/04 09.34

ATTN.MOHAMED

CONFIRM ACCEPTANCE OF ALI AKHBAR FOR 17B FROM 20 EEEE
02 JULY. ACCOMMODATION DETAILS TO FOLLOW.

BEST REGARDS

MARY

2

30/04 18.20
5839477PANDORA P
298574 STARLET 2

GOOD MORNING FROM STARLET – ASWAN

ATTN. MARY

I HAVE A BOOKING FOR COURSE 17B FROM 02/07 FOR 4 WEEKS.
THE STUDENT IS
MR ALI AKHBAR – AGED 27
H/B ACCM NEAR SCHOOL PLS
PLS CONFIRM
MANY TKS AND RGDS
MOHAMED/STARLET – ASWAN

5839477 PANDORA P
298574 STARLET 2

3

5839477PANDORA P

DEAR SIR,

I WOULD LIKE SOME INFORMATION ABOUT YOUR SUMMER COURSES
IN ENGLISH FOR ONE OF MY SONS FOR ONE MONTH, STARTING
AUGUST 2ND OR 3RD:
  – COST OF COURSE
  – POSSIBILITY OF ACCOMMODATION AND ITS COST
  – ASSISTANCE IN OBTAINING A TEMPORARY RESIDENCE PERMIT
   FOR THE PERIOD OF HIS STAY IN PANDORA, IF NECESSARY
   (BRAZILIAN NATIONALITY)
THANK YOU VERY MUCH FOR YOUR PROMPT REPLY TO TELEX NO. 49867
BKHO

BEST REGARDS
PAULO RUGGERO

5839477PANDORA P

4

BCO92 09.45
5839477PANDORA P
KEY + 33074545 + KZY
49867BKHO
5839477PANDORA P
PANDORA SCHOOL OF LANGUAGES
10/7/86

ATTN: PAULO RUGGERO

THANK YOU FOR YOUR TELEX.

WE HAVE A 4 WEEK COURSE BEGINNING 2 AUGUST, AND WE TAKE ADULTS
OVER THE AGE OF 18. COST OF 4 WEEKS IS 525 STG. ACCOMMODATION
IS EXTRA: APPROX. 50 PER WEEK FOR BED AND BREAKFAST IN FAMILY,
AND APPROX. 75 FOR BED, BREAKFAST AND DINNER.

IF WE RECEIVE DEFINITE CONFIRMATION OF BOOKING WE CAN SEND
CERTIFICATE OF ACCEPTANCE WHICH WILL ALLOW YOUR SON TO
ENTER THE COUNTRY AS A STUDENT FOR THE LENGTH OF HIS STAY
WITH US.

WE LOOK FORWARD TO HEARING FROM YOU.

BEST REGARDS
MARY PETERSEN/STUDENT OFFICER

5839477PANDORA P
49867BKHO

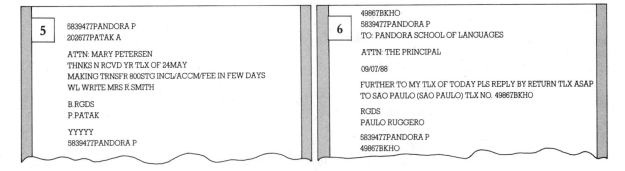

5

5839477PANDORA P
202677PATAK A

ATTN: MARY PETERSEN
THNKS N RCVD YR TLX OF 24MAY
MAKING TRNSFR 800STG INCL/ACCM/FEE IN FEW DAYS
WL WRITE MRS R.SMITH

B.RGDS
P.PATAK

YYYYY
5839477PANDORA P

6

49867BKHO
5839477PANDORA P
TO: PANDORA SCHOOL OF LANGUAGES

ATTN: THE PRINCIPAL

09/07/88

FURTHER TO MY TLX OF TODAY PLS REPLY BY RETURN TLX ASAP
TO SAO PAULO (SAO PAULO) TLX NO. 49867BKHO

RGDS
PAULO RUGGERO

5839477PANDORA P
49867BKHO

---

3 The Balmy Holiday Club Head Office is in Paris. Read the telex they sent to the Holiday Club in Bahamia.

> 459760 BALMY J
> 5839321 PARIS P
> 28.07 17.45
>
> ATTN: ELSWORTHY
> GLAD TO HEAR CAMP IS FULL. YES, DO TAKE ON ANOTHER
> ASSISTANT FROM 1 TO 31 AUGUST IF NECESSARY. SALARY
> 150 STG PER WEEK. ACCOMMODATION AND ALL FOOD FREE OF
> CHARGE. WORK HOURS MAXIMUM 8 PER DAY, ONE DAY PER
> WEEK HOLIDAY.
> HOW ARE ANNE MARSHALL AND TONY FIELD GETTING ON?
> KEEP UP THE GOOD WORK.
> MAX JOURDAIN/DIRECTOR BALMY HOLIDAYS
>
> 5839321 PARIS P
> 459760 BALMY J

Now answer these questions:

a Max Jourdain's telex is a reply to a telex sent by Jim Elsworthy.
Who do you think Jim is?
b What does Jim want to do?
c Look at the work conditions. Do you think it is a good job?
Discuss it with the other students.
d What do you think Jim said in the telex he sent to Max before this?

4 Now write the telex you think Jim wrote in reply to this telex.
Include this information:
a He thanks Max for his telex.
b He tells Max that one of Anne and Tony's friends is coming for an interview for the job.
c He tells Max how Anne and Tony are getting on.
d He asks Max if he can open a new bar because the old one is too small.

A Curriculum vitae (C.V.)

1 Richard wants a job as a camp assistant at the Balmy Holiday Club.
Look at his curriculum vitae and letter of application:

CURRICULUM VITAE

Name: RICHARD STANLEY WILTON

Address: 64 Arundel Road   Tel: 0642 – 916216
             Bradford, W.Yorks
             BL4 8NW

Date of Birth: 4 December 1960

Nationality: British

Marital Status: Single

Present Occupation: Photographer for *Wild Life* Magazine

Education and Qualifications

June 1976	G.C.E. O levels:	English, Maths, Physics, Chemistry, Geography
June 1978	G.C.E. A levels:	Geography, Maths
Oct. 1979 – June 1982	B.Sc. in Computer Science, Polytechnic of South London	
1985	Instructor's Diploma, Royal Tennis Association	

Experience

Summer 1980, 1981	Worked as Camp Assistant in Brinton's Holiday Camp, Lowestoft, U.K.
1982–1985	Computer Programmer, Blaxil Chemicals, Luton, U.K.
1986–1987	Travel Guide, Grecotours Ltd., Athens, Greece.
1987–present	Photographer, *Wild Life* Magazine

Languages: French – fair   Greek – good

Hobbies: Cinema, politics

Sports: Tennis: Qualified as Instructor in 1985
           Swimming, football, cricket, volleyball

Valid Driving Licence since 1978

References:

Mr James Francome	Mrs Jane Wilson
21 Manor Road	*Wild Life* Magazine
London SE14	17–21 Queen Street
U.K.	Bradford, W. Yorks.
(Tutor at Polytechnic)	U.K.
	(Editor of magazine)

---

64 Arundel Road
Bradford
W. Yorks.
BL4 8NW

25th May 19—

Personnel Officer
Balmy Holiday Club
White Sands
Bahamia

Dear Sir or Madam,

I have heard from a friend of mine, Tony Field, that you have vacancies for camp assistants at your camp in Bahamia. I would like to apply for the job.

As you will see from my curriculum vitae, I have worked in a hotel, and as a shop assistant. After leaving university in 1982, I worked for six years as a shop assistant in Luton. Then from 1984 to 1987, I was a pilot in Portugal. Since 1987, I have worked as a reporter for *Wild Life* Magazine.

I am very interested in sport, and I have been a qualified wind-surf instructor since 1985. I swim, and play rugby, cricket and volleyball. My other interests are cinema and politics. I have had a driving licence since 1985.

I would be grateful if you would consider my application.

I look forward to hearing from you.

Yours faithfully,

R. S. Wilton

RICHARD WILTON

2 Some of the information in Richard's letter is not correct. Compare the letter with his curriculum vitae. Underline the mistakes and discuss the correct details with your teacher.

B Writing a curriculum vitae

1 There are many different ways of writing a curriculum vitae (or C.V.). We give a basic model which will be useful for most situations

The C.V. is divided into 5 parts:
a Personal Information
b Education and Qualifications
c Experience
d Other (Hobbies, languages etc.)
e References

a Personal Information

Include:

full name (in capitals)
home address
address for correspondence (if it is different from home address)
telephone number (with dialling code)
date of birth
nationality
marital status
present occupation

b Education and Qualifications

In chronological order.

c Experience

You do not need to write every job you have ever done, but you must write all the jobs/experience which will help you in your job application.

d Other

Here you may include:

languages
sports
interests and hobbies etc
driving licence

e References

At least two; usually, one should be from your present employer.

2 Read this interview with Lisa Franks and complete the C.V. that follows.

Man: Good morning, Miss _____?
Lisa: Franks, Lisa Franks. Mrs, actually.
Man: Aha. And you're 24, is that right?
Lisa: Yes. My date of birth is 4th April, 1965.

Man: Good. Now, have you got an address where we can write to you?

Lisa: Yes: 128a Station Street, Perth, Scotland.

Man: Thank you. Now, tell me something about your experience in this kind of work, Mrs Franks.

Lisa: Well, I worked as a shop assistant for four years … at Super-stores in Perth.

Man: And when was that?

Lisa: I finished that in 1985. And then I worked as a trainee store manager in Perth for a year. …

Man: And the name of the store?

Lisa: MacVie's.

Man: And since then?

Lisa: Well, since 1986, I've been the store manager at Bloxham's in Stirling.

Man: And can you tell me about your qualifications?

Lisa: Certainly. I've got four O levels – French, English, Maths and Statistics.

Man: Any A levels?

Lisa: No.

Man: Anything else you can tell me?

Lisa: Yes, I can speak a little French.

Man: And your hobbies?

Lisa: Water-skiing – I love water-skiing. And swimming.

Man: I see, good. I'd like two references please.

Lisa: Yes, OK. There's my present boss, Mrs Mary Dalton. Would you like her address?

Man: Yes please.

Lisa: Area Manager, Bloxham's Stores, Bloxham House, High Street, Stirling, Scotland. And then Mr Iain McDonald, 66 The Rise, Perth, Scotland. He was my French teacher at school.

Man: OK, Mrs Franks – thank you very much. We'll telephone you as soon as possible. Have you got a telephone number?

Lisa: Yes – it's 55462. And the code for Perth is 0738.

Name: *ELISABETH FRANKS*

Title: _____

Address: _____

          _____

          _____

Tel: _____ Date of Birth: _____

Nationality: *BRITISH*

Education and Qualification:

June 1981 GCE O levels _____

                          _____

Experience:

1981 –   Shop Assistant, Superstores, Perth

    – 1986 _____

    – present _____

Languages: _____

Hobbies: _____

References:

1   2

4 Exercise

Now write a curriculum vitae for your favourite pop star, sportsman or woman or for yourself.

5 Look at the letter on page 65 and Lisa's C.V. and fill in the spaces:

128a _____

_____

Scotland

28th November 19--

J.Salisbury Ltd.
48 Rose Road
Glasgow
GL4 2TD

Dear _____,

I have seen your advertisement in the Glasgow Herald for

store managers, and I would like to _____ for the job.

As you will see _____, I have worked

in shops and stores since _____, when I left school.

My first job was with _____ in Perth. After

leaving them in _____, I worked for _____ of

Perth until 19_____, and then I joined Bloxham's in _____

as a store manager.

I have got four _____ – in French, English, _____ and

Statistics. I can speak _____ a little, and my

hobbies are _____ and _____.

I would be grateful if you would consider my application.

Yours _____,

Lisa Franks

Elisabeth Franks (Mrs)

C Writing about the past

1 Look at these examples:

   a I *have worked* as a computer programmer.
   b I *worked* as a travel guide from 1982 to 1985.
   c Since 1985, I *have worked* as a tennis instructor.
   d I *have had* this cold for a week!

2 Can you say why we sometimes use 'I worked' and sometimes 'I have worked'?

In sentence **a**, the past time is not stated. We know that he has worked as a computer programmer at some point in his life, but it is not important *when*. So we use 'I have worked'.

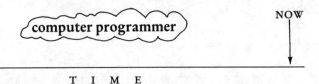

In sentence **b**, the period of time is given, and the period is finished. So we use 'I worked'.

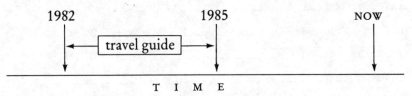

In sentences c and d, a period of time is given, and it is *not* finished. In **c**, for example, he is still working as a tennis instructor; in d, he still has a cold. So we use 'I have worked' or 'I have had'.

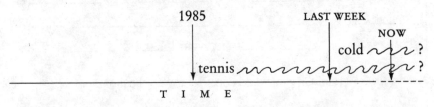

Key

      = completed past action, we *do not* know
        exactly when.

      = completed past action, we *know* when.

      = action started in the past, continues in the
        present and may continue in the future.

3 Practice

Choose the correct form in each sentence. Cross out the *wrong* form of the verb.

e.g. I went/~~have gone~~ to Paris last week.

a I lived/have lived in London from 1942 to 1948.
b I had/have had my present car for ten years.
c He arrived/has arrived yesterday.
d He worked/has worked at IBM since 1982.
e She went/has gone skating for the first time last week.
f I stayed/have stayed in Bahamia last summer.
g I lived/have lived in Brighton since 1942.
h Q What did she do when she was in Spain?
　　A She worked/has worked as a teacher.

4 Look at Susan's life:

Now fill in the blanks using the time-line to help you:

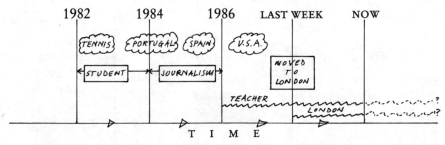

At the moment Susan is a teacher in London. She (live) _____ in London for a week because she (move) _____ there last Saturday. She (work) _____ as a teacher since 1986, but before that she (work) _____ in journalism for two years, from 1982 to 1984.

　　Susan has many interests and likes travelling. She (play) _____ tennis once or twice and she (go) _____ to Portugal, Spain and the U.S.A.

5 Now complete this time-line for your life. Do not write everything! You can invent things if you want to.

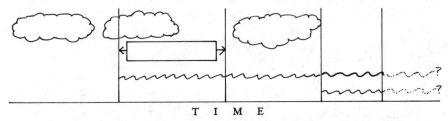

Now write a text about yourself. Look at the text about Susan to help you. You should base your text on your time-line.

When you have finished, give your text to your teacher, who will read out some of your descriptions. You should guess which student your teacher is reading about.

D Writing a letter of application for a job

1 Look at Unit 3, pages 19–21 to revise how to write a formal letter. Study the letter plan below. It tells you how to write an application letter for a job.

Your address

Today's date

The address of
the company

Dear _____

I am writing to apply for a position as shop assistant with your company. — Say why you are writing.

(As you will see from my C.V.) I worked as a _____ from 19— to 19— and since 19— I have worked as a _____ — Put your most important experience and your present job.

I have got _____ 'O' levels and _____ 'A' levels. I can speak Russian and French. I like cooking and jazz dancing. — Put your most important qualifications and other interests.

I look forward to hearing from you. — Greeting.

Yours (sincerely,
   (faithfully,

Paul Sprout

Paul Sprout (Mr)

— Ending and signature

2 Look at the two advertisements below:

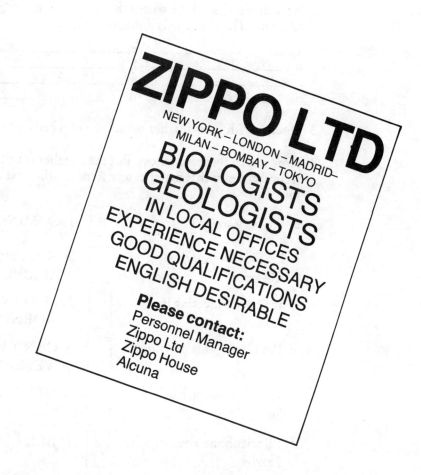

GROSVENOR HOTEL
needs
WAITERS
CLEANERS
KITCHEN STAFF
RECEPTIONISTS

Write to:
P. Walsh
Grosvenor Hotel
Grosvenor St
London WC1

ZIPPO LTD
NEW YORK – LONDON – MADRID–
MILAN – BOMBAY – TOKYO
BIOLOGISTS
GEOLOGISTS
IN LOCAL OFFICES
EXPERIENCE NECESSARY
GOOD QUALIFICATIONS
ENGLISH DESIRABLE

Please contact:
Personnel Manager
Zippo Ltd
Zippo House
Alcuna

Now write a letter applying for *one* of these jobs, based on the plan.
You can invent your experience and qualifications.

E Sending a telegram

1 Look at this telegram to Tony from his wife Jennie:

TELEGRAM TELEGRAM TELEGRAM TELEGRAM TELEGRAM

ARRIVING MONDAY 15.25 YORK TOWN
FLIGHT A2469 PLEASE MEET ME JENNIE

TELEGRAM TELEGRAM TELEGRAM TELEGRAM TELEGRAM

In telegrams we write the minimum we need to give the message. Jennie's telegram means:

'I am arriving on Monday at 15.25 at York Town airport on flight A2469. Please meet me.
Love Jennie.'

2 Now make a list of the words that are in the message but not in the telegram. The first one is done for you:

a _____I_____   e _____
b _____   f _____
c _____   g _____
d _____   h _____

3 Discuss with your teacher what type of words are omitted and why.

4 Now match these sentences. Put the number for the sentence in the second column that matches a sentence in the first column. **a** is done for you.

a I'm very sorry	7	1 COMING BACK SUNDAY
b I can't visit you this weekend		2 WILL PHONE WHEN ARRIVE
c as I have a meeting in Paris.		3 LEAVING THIS MORNING
d I'm leaving this morning		4 CAN'T VISIT THIS WEEKEND
e and I'm coming back on Sunday.		5 MEETING IN PARIS
f I'll telephone you when I arrive.		6 JILL
g With best wishes, from Jill		7 SORRY

5 Now write a telegram to give this message. Remember to use only the words which give important information. You will need about eighteen words:

> I am sorry but I can't meet you on Monday because I am working at the Club at the time you arrive. I suggest you take a taxi to the Club. Could you please bring my blue sun-glasses with you?
> From Tony.

6 Now compare your telegram with the one written by your partner. Are they the same?

7 Discuss with your teacher when you might want to send a telegram.

8 Here are some messages from telegrams. Put the name of the person in the space:

a _____ is 21 years old today.
b _____ is going abroad on business.
c _____ are getting married today.
d _____ has just finished university and got a degree.
e _____ 's father has just died.
f _____ is in hospital.
g _____ does not want to receive the goods he has ordered.

> MARY
> CONGRATULATIONS ON YOUR SUCCESS
>
> LOVE SUE

> GRANDMA
> GET BETTER SOON HOPE
> TO VISIT NEXT MONDAY
> MUCH LOVE JENNY

> MR ALEXANDER
> REGRET CANT MEET YOU
> THURSDAY URGENT SUMMONS
> TO TOKYO FROM HEAD OFFICE
> WILL PHONE TUESDAY
> REGARDS TIM AINSLEY

> ELSPETH
> HAPPY BIRTHDAY
> PRESENT FOLLOWING
> LOVE JO

> TONY
> SO SORRY TO HEAR YOUR NEWS
> THINKING OF YOU WITH DEEPEST
> SYMPATHY LOVE MARIA

> MAKEWELL LTD
> REGRET MUST CANCEL ORDER DUE TO
> UNEXPECTED CHANGE OF PLANS
> LETTER FOLLOWING REGARDS
> P.BROWNWELL – STOCKSLEY LTD

> JACK AND LIZ
> CONGRATULATIONS AND BEST WISHES
> FOR FUTURE HAPPINESS
> MUCH LOVE MARK

A Looking towards the future

1 Tony's wife, Jennie, is travelling to Bahamia to visit him at the Balmy Holiday Club where he is working. On the plane she meets Richard, a friend of Tony's, and they talk. Read the conversation between Jennie and Richard.

Jennie: Oh, hello, you're Richard ... aren't you?

Richard: Oh, hello, yes ... now, I remember you – you're Jennie, yes, that's right. Jennie – Tony's wife.

Jennie: Yes, I am. I've got two weeks' holiday so I'm going to Bahamia to visit him – but why are you going to Bahamia?

Richard: Well, it's a long story really, but I'm looking for a job and Tony wrote to me about the Holiday Club – they were looking for staff. I wrote back and, well – here I am. I'm going to work there for one or two months and then I'm going to travel for the rest of the year. I decided to do that this year and then next year I'm going to look for a more permanent job. What about you? Are you just going to visit Tony or have you got any other plans?

Jennie: Well, actually ... yes ... I have. I'm going to stay with Tony for a week in White Sands, but then I'm going to go skiing on Mount Gunne ...

Answer these questions:

a Who are Jennie and Richard?   c What are their plans?
b Where are they?

2 Look at these two sentences. What is the difference?

a *I'm going to Bahamia to visit him.*
b *I'm going to work there for one or two months.*

In sentence a 'go' is the main verb. Jennie is talking about the present.

In sentence b 'go' is an auxiliary. It shows that it is his *intention* to work there in the future, not now.

3 Read the conversation again, and make a list of Richard's intentions and a list of Jennie's intentions like this. The first one is done for you.

Richard's intentions
a He is going to work at Balmy Holidays for one or two months.
b
c

Jennie's intentions
a
b
c

4 Study the time-line below with your teacher. It shows Richard's intentions.

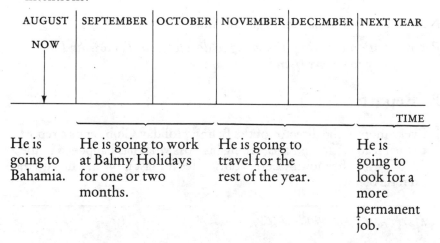

AUGUST	SEPTEMBER	OCTOBER	NOVEMBER	DECEMBER	NEXT YEAR
NOW					

TIME

He is going to Bahamia.   He is going to work at Balmy Holidays for one or two months.   He is going to travel for the rest of the year.   He is going to look for a more permanent job.

5 Look at these time-lines for Julie and Peter. They are two friends who meet on the train to London.

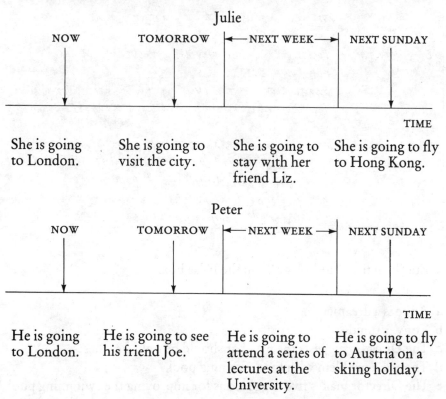

Julie

NOW   TOMORROW   ◄—NEXT WEEK—►   NEXT SUNDAY

TIME

She is going to London.   She is going to visit the city.   She is going to stay with her friend Liz.   She is going to fly to Hong Kong.

Peter

NOW   TOMORROW   ◄—NEXT WEEK—►   NEXT SUNDAY

TIME

He is going to London.   He is going to see his friend Joe.   He is going to attend a series of lectures at the University.   He is going to fly to Austria on a skiing holiday.

6 Now, with the help of the conversation (1) on page 76, write what Julie says when they meet on the train.

Begin like this:
Julie: *Oh hello Peter. How are you?*
Peter: *I'm fine thanks, and you? What are you doing here?*
Julie: *Well, I'm going to London to do a lot of things really. Tomorrow I'm going to visit the city and then ...*

Now write Peter's answer. Begin like this:

Peter: *That's interesting. I'm going to do a lot, too. Tomorrow I'm going to see my friend Joe.*

B Reports

1 Every month, the director of the Balmy Holiday Club sends a report to the Head Office in Paris, telling his boss what has happened in the Club during the month. Look at his notes for last month. Then do the exercise below.

MONTHLY REPORT NOTES

1. New staff   ANNE   Positive: works hard. People like her.
    Negative: Sometimes late. Dreams a lot.

    TONY   Positive: works hard. Negative: a bit shy.

2. New bar   Positive: working well. Guests using bar –
    not town bars
    Suggestion: – one evening a week – open to public
    for "Cocktail Evening" – guests meet locals

3. Swimming Pool – Nobody's using it! A disaster – why?
    1. Atmosphere rather cold – put in more grass and trees.
    2. Water looks dirty – paint pool white.
    3. People don't know about it – More events:
    water polo – swimming galas !

Write 'T' in the True box or 'F' in the False box.

TRUE   FALSE

☐   ☐   **a** Anne is a dreamer.
☐   ☐   **b** Tony is timid.
☐   ☐   **c** The Director suggests the new bar should be only for guests.
☐   ☐   **d** There is a problem with the swimming pool.
☐   ☐   **e** The Director makes five suggestions for improving the swimming pool.

2 Now look at the report below, and fill in the gaps with words from the box. Look again at the notes at B1, page 78, to help you.

punctual	late	dirty
cold	well	hard
better	trees	three
using	white	popular
problem	dreamer	shy

BALMY HOLIDAY CLUB – BAHAMIA
Monthly Report – Confidential

1 New Staff: Anne Marshall, Tony Field

POSITIVE
Both Anne and Tony work _____ and well. Anne is very _____ with the guests and also very well organised. Tony is perhaps not as popular as Anne. However, he is very _____ and conscientious.

NEGATIVE
Although Anne works hard and the guests like her, she is sometimes _____, and this is probably because she is a _____. However, she is a very likeable girl. Tony works very well, but he is not as popular, because he is rather _____.

2 New Bar
The new cocktail bar is working _____ and the guests use it more than the town bars. However, it could work _____ perhaps if we organised a 'public' Cocktail Evening one night a week, so that guests can meet some of the local people.

3 Swimming Pool
Unfortunately we have a serious _____ with the swimming pool: not many guests are _____ it, and prefer to go to the town pool, or to the beach. There are _____ reasons for this: first, the atmosphere in the pool is rather _____; next, although the water is very clean, it *looks* _____; finally, some guests don't even know it exists!
I have three suggestions:
1 Plant more grass and _____ around the pool to make it more friendly.
2 Paint the inside of the pool _____ in place of the present blue.
3 Hold more events in the swimming pool: swimming competitions, water polo matches etc.

C Conjunctions

1

BUT	ALTHOUGH	HOWEVER

Look at these examples:

> The hotel was not luxurious *but* it was clean.
> *Although* the hotel was clean, it was not luxurious.
> The hotel was clean. *However*, it was not luxurious.

These three conjunctions link positive and negative ideas. What are the differences in the ways they are used? Discuss with your teacher.

2 Look at the Balmy Holiday Club 'Comments' sheet, where visitors can write their criticism or praise.

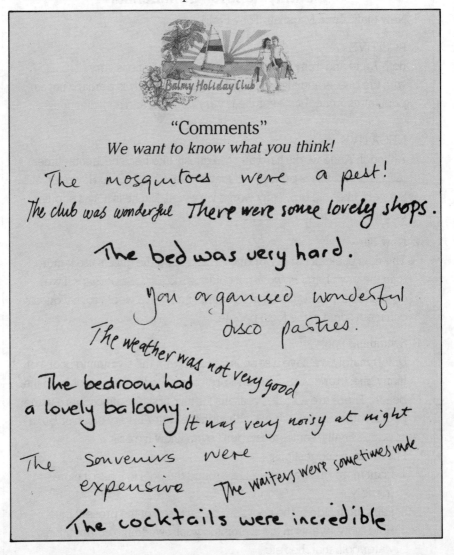

"Comments"
We want to know what you think!

The mosquitoes were a pest!

The club was wonderful. There were some lovely shops.

The bed was very hard.

You organised wonderful disco parties.

The weather was not very good

The bedroom had a lovely balcony.

It was very noisy at night

The souvenirs were expensive

The waiters were sometimes rude.

The cocktails were incredible

The comments are negative and positive. Write them in the correct categories. The first is done for you.

Positive

a *The club was wonderful.*

Negative

a *The weather was not very good.*

3 Now link these sentences using 'but', 'although' and 'however'. Find two examples for each conjunction. The first one is done for you.

a *The club was wonderful* but *the weather was not very good.*

4 Because

'Because' explains the reason for something.

Look at the example:

> *The town is dirty because there is a lot of traffic.*

Complete the following sentences in any way you like, giving reasons. The first one is done for you:

1 The weather in Sudan is hot because **it is near the Equator.**
2 Mary is very tired because ...
3 The boy stayed in hospital for two weeks because ...
4 They didn't go to the cinema because ...
5 Tom got a lot of presents because ...
6 He was late for his appointment because ...

Compare your answers with those of other students. How many different reasons did you think of?

5 So

'So' expresses the result of something. Look at the example.

> *There is a lot of traffic so the town is dirty.*

Now complete these sentences, giving the result:

1 I don't feel very well this morning so **I'm going to stay at home ...**
2 The water in the swimming pool is very cold so ...
3 She loves skiing so ...
4 The two boys come from a very poor family so ...
5 Mary loves reading so ...
6 He can't see very well so ...

Now compare your answers with those of other students. How many results did you think of?

6 Write some incomplete sentences ending in 'because' or 'so' on a piece of paper. Give the sentences to your partner to complete.

D Comparatives

Hilda – 30 years old

Hilda She has a lot of good friends and likes going to parties. She often works hard but she likes relaxing too. She is a good cook. She is always late. She does not like sport.

Mavis – 28 years old

Mavis Mavis has some good friends. She loves cooking, working at home and reading. She is not very punctual. She hates sport.

1 Look at the pictures and read the information about Hilda and Mavis. Now look at these adjectives and write out correct lists for Hilda or Mavis. The first one is done for you.

happy	good cook	very bad at sport
always very late	very dark hair	very hard-working
very good cook	often late	dark hair
bad at sport	very fat	very happy
very popular	young	fat
hard-working	popular	young

HILDA   MAVIS
fat   *very fat*

ADJECTIVE + **ER** = COMPARATIVE

a one-syllable words: → **ER**
old → old**er** *Hilda's hair is darker than Mavis's.*

b one-syllable words ending in single vowel + single consonant:
  double consonant + **ER**
  hot → hot**ter** _____

c two-syllable words ending in 'y': y → **i** + **ER**
  noisy → nois**ier** _____

d one-syllable words ending in 'e': e → **ER**
  nice → nic**er** _____

MORE + ADJECTIVE = COMPARATIVE

e two or more syllables: → **more** + ADJECTIVE
  boring → **more** boring _____
  interesting → **more** interesting _____

IRREGULAR ADJECTIVES

f Adjectives with special comparative forms
  good → **better** _____
  bad → **worse** _____

Now write these sentences in the correct section. The first is done for you:

Hilda's hair is *darker* than Mavis's.
Mavis is *worse* at sport than Hilda.
Hilda is *more popular* than Mavis.
Mavis is a *better* cook than Hilda.
Mavis is *happier* than Hilda.
Hilda is always *later* than Mavis.
Mavis is *fatter* than Hilda.

3 Look at the notes for Reports in B1 on page 78 and complete this text using the correct comparative forms of the adjectives.

Anne is a hard worker and Tony is, too, but although people like him, Anne is (popular) _____. He is a bit shy and Anne is (confident) _____. Anne is often (late) _____ than Tony, because she dreams a lot, and he is (punctual) _____.

Tony and Anne like the Balmy Holiday Club, but at the moment Anne is (happy) _____ than Tony because she has met a lot of new people. She likes to go out and socialise a lot, but Tony is (quiet) _____ than Anne and prefers to stay at the Club when he is free. He also likes sports and is (good) _____ at swimming and tennis than Anne, who prefers drinking cocktails.

4 Now choose two students in your class. Call them student X and student Y, and write a short description of them. See if the others can guess who they are. Your first sentence might look like this:

Student X has fair hair and is a bit taller than student Y.

5

JAMES   PATRICK   BETSY   LAURA

a James is as tall as Patrick.
b Betsy is not as tall as Laura.
c Laura is taller than Betsy.

What are the rules for '(not) as _____ as' and 'than'?
Look at the pictures and discuss them with your teacher.

Complete the sentences with 'as' or 'than'. Look again at D1, page 82.

a Mavis is younger _____ Hilda.
b Mavis is not as popular _____ Hilda.
c Hilda is as pretty _____ Mavis.
d Hilda is more popular _____ Mavis.
e Hilda is not as hard-working _____ Mavis.
f Mavis is as intelligent _____ Hilda.

Now complete these sentences:

g The U.S.A. is bigger _____ Britain.
h Greece is not as rich _____ Germany.
i Spain is as hot _____ Italy in the summer.
j The Nile is longer _____ the Mississippi.
k Milk is not as expensive _____ caviar.
l Tennis is as popular _____ golf in Britain.
m Women are usually smaller _____ men.

E Ordering your ideas – marking words

1 When you are writing a report, it is important to be as clear as possible. If you want to make a list of different ideas, it is a good idea to introduce these ideas with marking words.

Marking words: 'first', 'second', 'next', 'finally'.

Look at this paragraph:

> There are three main reasons for the success of Bahamia Steels Plc. First, they have a young dynamic Managing Director. Next, they have introduced new technology in all parts of the company – this has reduced costs and increased efficiency. Finally, they have a permanent contract with the Bahamian government, which buys 50% of their output.

Why is Bahamia Steels so successful? Write three sentences.

2 a Why do you like your town? England?   b Why don't you like your town? England?

Choose question **a** or **b** and write three reasons.

Now complete this paragraph:

There are three reasons why I _____

_____. First, _____

_____. Next, _____

_____. Finally, _____

_____.

3 In Bahamia, the government has to choose between building more roads or more railways. Look at the notes of the Minister of Transport:

> Why build more roads?
> 1 We need good roads for tourists.
> 2 Will make it possible to reach isolated parts of island.
> 3 People with cars will vote for us.

> Why build more railways?
> 1 Railways are used by *all* the people, not only those with cars.
> 2 Much safer.
> 3 They will create new jobs.

What would you do? Build more roads or build more railways? Now choose one set of notes only and write a paragraph based on them. Look at the paragraph at E1, above, for help.

F Writing a report

1 Look again at the notes about the Balmy Holiday Club at B1, page 78. Make similar notes about the place where you work or study. Choose three things from list A to discuss, and write them in the spaces marked 1, 2, 3. Then choose adjectives from list B to describe them. Write suggestions in the spaces marked 'Suggestion'.

List A

people
work/job/study
equipment
building
conditions
timetable
work/school life

List B

POSITIVE	NEGATIVE
friendly	noisy
helpful	shy
interesting	difficult
varied	boring
available	long
easy to use	cold
comfortable	hot
well-organised	badly organised
enjoyable	old-fashioned
modern	
flexible	

YOUR NOTES

List A

1 _____

2 _____

3 _____

List B

Positive: _____

_____

Negative: _____

_____

Suggestion: _____

_____

Positive: _____

_____

Negative: _____

_____

Suggestion: _____

_____

Positive: _____

_____

Negative: _____

_____

Suggestion: _____

_____

2 Now use your notes to write a report for a local magazine. Write three paragraphs. Remember to use the conjunctions you have practised and the comparative forms if necessary. Use 'first', 'second', 'next' and 'finally' to order your ideas. Look at the report at B2, page 79 to help you.

A Formal invitations

1 Look at the invitation and answer the questions:

a Who is the invitation to?
b Who is getting married?
c Who is Mr James Marshall?
d When and where is the wedding?
e What do you think R.S.V.P. means?

> Mr and Mrs James Marshall
>
> request the pleasure of the company of
>
> *Peter Robinson*
> _____
>
> at the marriage of their daughter Anne to Mr Gary Suarez.
> On Saturday 12 December 19–– at 3.00 p.m.
> At St. James's Church, Highgate.
>
> 'The Lodge'
> Park Road
> Amersham
> Bucks.   R.S.V.P.

2 a

> Mr and Mrs James Marshall
> request the pleasure of the company of

b

> Dear Peter,
>   Would you like to come to Annes Wedding .....

Look at these two invitations (**a** and **b**). What is the difference? In what situations would you use them? Discuss with your teacher.

3 Sometimes we are invited to formal occasions, such as weddings, business meetings, conferences, lunches or dinners. The language used in these invitations is different from the language in informal invitations (see page 37).

Here are five formal invitations. Match the number of the invitation with the description (put the correct number in the boxes below):

a Invitation to a wedding ☐
b Invitation to a drinks party ☐
c Invitation to a lecture ☐
d Invitation to a charity lunch ☐
e Invitation to a dinner party ☐

1

17 Midstreet
Great Barmouth
Lincs.
16th March 19—

Dear Mr and Mrs Jones,

My husband and I would be very pleased if you could join us for dinner on Thursday evening at about 7.00.

Yours sincerely,

Mary Allen

2

THE ROYAL SOCIETY FOR
THE PREVENTION OF CRUELTY TO CATS
is holding its
ANNUAL LUNCHEON
in the Town Hall on Saturday 4th March
To reserve your place, please complete
and return the form below:

I/We would like to reserve _____ places
for the RSPCC Luncheon on 4th March
at 1.00p.m. I/We enclose a cheque
for the sum of _____ (£30 per person)
Return to: Mrs J. Peace, 101 High St, Lincoln.

3

*David and Lucy Smith
would like to
invite you to their
HOUSE WARMING
on Saturday 8th March
from 6.00 to 8.00 p.m.
and look forward to showing you
their new home.*

R.S.V.P.

4

Monday 5th June – 17.00 hrs

Dr David Holby
will be speaking on the subject of
German Literature from 1400 to 1500
in the New Arts Studio. All members
of the Literary Society are cordially
invited to attend.

MR and MRS JAMES ROBINSON

request the pleasure of the company of

_____

at the marriage of their daughter Rachel
to Mr Jacob Luder
On Saturday 4th April 19— at 2 p.m.
At St. Peter's Church, Church Street

"Lakeside"
Prince Road
Cambridge

R.S.V.P.

4 Formal replies

Look at these replies and discuss them with your teacher:

a

> Dear Tom,
> Thank you very much for your invitation.
>
> I will be very happy to come, and look forward to seeing you on Thursday at 8.00.
>
> Yours,
>
> *Susan*

b

> Dear Anne,
>
> Thank you very much for your invitation.
>
> I am afraid I will not be able to come as
> I have an important meeting that day.   **(or)**
> it is my mother's birthday and we are
>   having a family party.   **(or)**
> my sister has to go into hospital.   **(or)**
> my wife is expecting a baby that week.
>
> I hope to see you soon.   **(or)**
> I hope you have a good time.   **(or)**
> I will telephone you next week.
>
> With my very best wishes,
>
> *Peter*

Which reply says 'Yes' to the invitation and which one says 'No'?

5 Now read this invitation and write Richard's reply. You will find all the words in box **b**. Did he say 'Yes' or 'No'?

a

> John and Mary Folkes
> are happy to invite
> *Richard Wilton*
> ─────────────
>
> to an informal cocktail
> party at Hardside Hall
> at 8 p.m. on Saturday
> 22nd November.
>
> R.S.V.P.
> to Hardside Hall

b

and Mr Thank to I Folkes your
going be not Richard afraid come to much
Paris Yours, am as invitation for wishes
weekend Mrs you I very will that able
best With Wilton I am Dear

6 Look again at the invitations at A3, page 89. Choose one event – a wedding, lunch, drinks party, etc. Imagine you are organising it. Write a formal invitation to this event, and invite your partner. Remember to write where and when it will be. You want a reply, so do not forget to write R.S.V.P.

Now give your invitation to your partner. He/she will give his/hers to you. Read the invitation and write a reply. Give this to your partner.

B Narrative

1 Read this letter quickly. It does not matter if you do not understand all the words.

Balmy Holiday Club
White Sands
Bahamia
29th August 19--

Dear Julie,

How are you? I'm sorry I haven't written for so long but so much has happened recently! It's difficult to know where to start.

Well, you know that Tony and I decided to come to Bahamia on holiday three months ago. We were discussing it in the pub when you arrived with Mike, remember? Well, in any case, we came, as you know, because I sent you a postcard from Pandora, didn't I?

Although Pandora is a beautiful little village with interesting things to see, our hotel wasn't very good, and we could only find expensive restaurants. So we thought we could either go home, or find somewhere else, and that's what we did.

About a week after we arrived on the island we came to White Sands and discovered Balmy Holidays, who, luckily, were looking for new staff. Well, that was it. We applied for the jobs, and a week later we started working here, and we've been here since then.

Well, things were going quite well, except for Tony - he's so boring! However, I remembered my pen-friend Gary, who lives in Pandora. I tried to meet him when we were there, but couldn't. So we arranged to meet here and he came to White Sands for a Club disco. Anyway, we liked each other, and we've seen each other regularly for the last three weeks. So my news is .... you've guessed! We're going to get married in December, in England. I hope you'll come. I'll send you an official invitation later. Well, that's it for the moment. Write and tell me what you think.

Lots of love,

Anne

2 Look at the table below. With the help of Anne's letter, put the letters identifying the sentences (A, B, C, etc.) in the corresponding places on the time-line. Your teacher will help you. The first is done for you.

TIMELINE

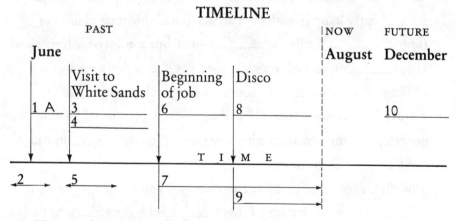

A Tony and I decided to come to Bahamia.
B They were looking for new staff.
C We came to White Sands.
D We discovered Balmy Holidays.

E We were discussing it in the pub when you
   arrived with Mike.
F We've been here since then.
G We started working here.
H We've seen each other regularly for the last
   three weeks.
I Gary came to White Sands for a Club
   disco.
J We're going to get married in December.

3 In pairs, with the help of the table in 2, discuss the different rules for
  when you use these tenses:

  a Simple Past: 'We *decided* to come to Bahamia three months ago.'
  b Present Perfect: 'We've *been* here since then.'
  c Past Continuous: 'They *were looking* for new staff.'
  d Going to: 'We're *going to* get married in December.'

  Now discuss the rules with your teacher.

4 On a piece of paper, write a question using 'you' for each of the tenses
  listed in part 3. For example:

  a *When did you first go abroad?*

  Then put your piece of paper in the 'postbox' your teacher will bring.
  Take another piece of paper from the box and write answers to the
  questions on it.

5 Look at this story and put the correct forms of the verbs in the spaces:

  When I (be) _____ a child, things (be) _____ very different. I (live)
  _____ fairly happily with my parents like all the other children I
  (know) _____. We (have) _____ a small but comfortable house and
  I (go) _____ to school, which I (not like) _____ very much.

  Then, when I (be) _____ fourteen, my parents (get) _____
  divorced. I will never forget how they told me. I (study) _____
  geography in my bedroom when my mother (come) _____ in and
  (tell) _____ me the news.

  Well, life (go) _____ on for another two years. Then, when I (be)
  _____ sixteen, (at that time I (live) _____ with my father), he (tell)
  _____ me some more news. This time, when he (tell) _____ me, I
  (study) _____ German. I remember exactly what I (write) _____.
  It (be) _____ a translation of Kafka. Well, of course, the news (be)
  _____ that he (want) _____ to get married again, and his new wife
  (have) _____ two small children, so I would have to leave school

and start working because there would not be enough money.

I (cannot) _____ believe it, but I (see) _____ that he really (want) _____ to get married, and so I (agree) _____. Well, that (be) _____ three years ago, and I (find) _____ a job as a secretary and translator in an office near my home.

I (work) _____ there since then and I suppose I should be happy because I (use) _____ my languages often in the last year and I (save) _____ some money too. Life at home is not perfect because I (not like) _____ children very much, but it (be not) _____ really difficult – just boring!

And so next year I (move) _____ into my own flat and I (study) _____ at night school. Or perhaps a handsome prince on a beautiful white horse will save me!

C Consolidation

1 Make notes about your life, interests and work under these categories:

   a Think of a change that you have made in your life, work or interests. (For example, in Anne's letter the big change was that she started a new job in Bahamia.)

   b How did the change happen? What were you doing when it happened? Why did it happen? (Anne was on holiday on the island and she went to White Sands when Balmy Holidays were looking for someone to employ.)

   c How have things progressed since then? (Anne tells Julie that the job has been all right but she has had problems with Tony, and she has seen a lot of Gary.)

   d What are your intentions for the future? (Anne is going to get married.)

2 On a piece of paper, write either a letter, or a section of your diary, or a report using these notes. Remember to use paragraphs, the correct tenses and conjunctions – for example: 'and', 'although', 'because', 'but', 'especially', 'however', 'so', 'when', 'while'. Do *not* write your name on the paper.

3 Give your paper to your teacher, who will give you a different one to read. Read it and guess who wrote it.

4 Tell the class who you think wrote the exercise and why you think so.

5 Tenses consequences (See Unit 5, part B5, page 40)

Take a big piece of paper. Think of two people, a man and a woman
(famous people, or students in the class). Think what they were doing
when they met and think of a place where they met, a question he
asked her beginning 'Have you ever . . . ?' and her reply. Think of
what they did after that and what is going to happen as a result.
At the top of the piece of paper write the man's name and what he was
doing. Then fold what you have written over, and pass the paper to
the student on your right. Take the paper from the student on your
left and write the woman's name and what she was doing on the new
piece of paper. Then fold it over again, pass it on and continue.

FOLD . . .	(Male name) was doing something
FOLD . . .	and (female name) was doing something
FOLD . . .	when they met at/in (a place).
FOLD . . .	He said, '_____' (Question with Have you ever . . . .?)
FOLD . . .	She replied, '_____'
FOLD . . .	So they _____ (what they did)
	and _____ (what they are going to do as a result of the story).

When you have finished, unfold the piece of paper and read out
your stories. They can be very funny!

To the teacher

What is this book?

In recent years the tendency in English language teaching has been to focus on the oral/aural component. However, there are many people all over the world who also need to communicate with others through writing. In this book we aim to build up the skills necessary to enable elementary students to carry out successfully such tasks as filling in forms and writing both informal and formal letters, telegrams, telexes, reports, postcards, curriculum vitaes, job applications and invitations.

Who is it for?

The material is aimed at elementary students who have completed about fifty hours of study before starting the course. It is designed to work as a separate writing course but can also be successfully integrated into a general English programme.

How is the book organised?

Each of the ten units prepares the students to carry out particular tasks in English. The language required is built up throughout the unit, with sections on specific grammar work, such as the use of tenses, comparatives, etc., and sections on skills development, such as punctuation, paragraphing, letter lay-out, etc. The development of the language is carefully graded and the order of presentation of the structures will correspond to that found in many elementary coursebooks. Teachers using the material as a supplement to a general English course may therefore find it useful as revision.

The underlying story-line will help to motivate students and provide continuity for those who use the book from beginning to end. However, an understanding of the story is not an essential requirement for use of the book, and many teachers will prefer to choose the sections they use according to the requirements of their class.

How is the book written?

Three basic principles underlie the way this book has been written. Firstly, that students should be encouraged to **communicate**. This means that many of the activities involve some kind of interaction with other students – sending messages, writing notes and letters, or exchanging information. This both requires and encourages a co-operative atmosphere in the classroom as students work in pairs and small groups.

Secondly, students who are encouraged to think about the nature of English are more likely to become successful in its use. For this reason, the teacher should try to elicit principles and ideas from the students rather than giving them the necessary information and hoping they will learn it. The questions in the book are designed to promote class discussion, which should enable teachers to guide students towards a fuller understanding of the material presented.

The third principle is that students will be more highly motivated and therefore more successful in their learning when they are given the freedom to write about what concerns them as individuals. We have therefore included a number of activities where students are encouraged to write about their own experience.

How should the book be used?

We have provided detailed notes to accompany each unit, giving suggested methods of presentation for many of the activities. There is also a key giving the answers to exercises for students working on their own.

TEACHER'S NOTES

Unit 1

Filling in forms, Titles in English, Punctuation 1, Exercise: Filling in an application form.

In the first unit students are introduced to Tony and Anne, two of the main characters in the story of Bahamia.

A Filling in forms

Before you introduce the characters, explain that in English-speaking countries most people have one surname/family name (which comes from the father) and one, two or three first names/Christian names. You may like to compare this system with that used in the country/countries of origin of your students. Then introduce Tony and Anne and go through the information presented in the forms. You may use this phase of the lesson to revise basic questions about identity, using the following procedure:

1 Ask the following questions about Tony:
What's his surname?
What's his title?
What are his first names? (Note that 'Tony' is an abbreviation of 'Anthony'.)
Look at his home address. (Explain that this is his permanent address – where his parents live.)
What's the name of his house?/road?/town?/county?/country?
(It is important for future activities that the students understand how the address is structured.)
Where does he live now? (Explain that as he is a student, this is only a temporary address.)
What's the name of his road?/town?/county?/country?
What's his telephone number at his home address?/present address?
How old is he?
What sex is he? (Teach the words 'male' and 'female'.)
What does he do?
When was he born? (Students should calculate the year of his birth and write it in on the form.)
Where was he born?
What's his nationality?
Is he married?
What are his interests?
What's the form for?

2 Point out the following equivalents:

Surname = Family name
First names = Other names = Forenames = Christian names
Block capitals = Capital letters
Telephone = Tel. No. = Tel.

Students go through the form about Anne, asking questions first across the class, then in pairs.

3 Explain to students how to complete exercises **a** and **b**, using the categories below the exercises and referring to the forms. This can be done in pairs.

Check exercise, preferably using an overhead projector (O.H.P.).

B Titles in English

Read through the titles in part 1. Explain that women can choose to be called 'Ms' or 'Mrs' if they are married, and 'Ms' or 'Miss' if they are single, as they prefer. Students fill in their own titles in part 1 and fill in parts 3 and 4 for themselves. Explain 'divorced' and 'widowed'.

C Punctuation

1 Demonstrate the different punctuation marks on the board.

3 Allow students to work in pairs to answer the questions, before going through the answers with the whole class. Point out that:

a Capital letters are used in English:
at the beginning of a sentence.
for the word 'I'.
for names of people.
for names of places (towns, countries).
for nationalities.
for months.
for days of the week.

b Full stops are used:
at the end of sentences.

c Apostrophes are used:
for abbreviations e.g. does not = doesn't, I am = I'm.
in the Saxon genitive to signal possession e.g. my wife's name.

d Question marks are used:
at the end of questions.

e Commas are used:
to divide a descriptive phrase from the noun which it describes e.g.
Glantree, a small town . . .

to divide two clauses of equal importance where there is a natural pause.

e.g. She's Scottish too, and her parents live in Edinburgh.

4 Students write out the exercise with the correct punctuation.

D Balmy Holiday Club – Application form

Pre-teach 'Marital status' and explain it can be 'single', 'widowed', 'divorced', etc.

Students fill in the application form for themselves or their partners. This exercise can be done as a role-play. One student is the travel agent, the other is the prospective traveller. In this case, pre-teach 'How would you like to pay?', 'By cash', 'By cheque', 'Sign here please'.

Unit 2

Location, Family, Introducing yourself, Informal letters.

A Location

1 This exercise can be done in pairs. Pre-teach the word 'resort'. Students match the descriptions with the names on the map. You then point to Bridlingpool and give the model sentence:

'This is Bridlingpool, a large port in the north of the island.' Students practise this and other sentences using the same structure. They should be encouraged to point to the place they are describing as they say the sentence. Students then complete part 2.

3 Draw students' attention to the rules about articles and prepositions, using the model sentences to elicit/explain that:

We use 'an' before a vowel. (Except for words beginning with ju: a university, a union, etc.)

We use 'a' before consonants including 'h'. (You may wish to point out the most common exception – 'an hour'.)

We use 'the' when the article refers to something of which there is only one: e.g. 'the capital'.

Note the omission of the article before the plural noun 'rivers'.

Demonstrate the use of prepositions. You may use a map on the blackboard to demonstrate the difference between 'north east of' and 'in the north east of'. Give students further practice in the use of articles and prepositions using the names of local places as prompts before allowing them to do the exercise.

Point out that in the exercise they must circle the dash ⊖ if no word is required. It may be useful to draw or put up a map of Britain showing the items named.

4 Students are required to fill in details on the map in their partner's book, inventing names for the sea, island, towns, etc., and then to write a description of the island prepared by their partner in their own book. Note that this is *not* an information gap exercise. Point out that when students are inventing names *they should follow the English rule of Adjective + Noun*. In this way you should avoid such inventions as 'sea green' 'island beautiful' and 'mountain white'!

B Family

Check again that students understand 'widower', 'divorced' and the irregular plural 'children'.

1 The first examples should be done orally before allowing students to complete the exercise in writing.

C Introducing yourself

1 Use the exercise to revise the present tense of the verbs 'be', 'have', 'live', 'like' and 'want'. You may need to give suggestions or discuss the exercise with the class before allowing them to write their own descriptions.

Point out that Richard uses 'I'm' and 'I've' because he is speaking. The written forms are 'I am' and 'I have'. The third person is 'she/he, is/has', and students should also notice the '-s' on the third person singular of verbs in the present tense.

3 For this activity the teacher needs a box/hat/bag in which to collect the forms once the students have completed them. If your students are all of the same age and nationality, adapt the exercise by asking students to write details of one of their parents, relatives or friends.

Point out that students of different ages can answer the questions as it suits them.

You will need to teach such constructions as:
'He/she is x metres tall', 'His/her hair is blonde/dark, etc.', 'Her/his favourite pop-star is x', 'He/she is left-(right)handed', 'She/he has one/two brothers/sisters', 'She/he has no brothers or sisters'. Point out the negative forms 'He hasn't got . . .' and 'He has no . . .' The former is more informal and usually used in spoken English, while the latter is more common in written English.

D Informal letters

1 Pre-teach the word 'pen-friend'. It may also be necessary to introduce the prepositions 'from' and 'to', using another letter to demonstrate: 'This letter is from/to X.'

The students should then be able to answer the four focus questions and you may add further questions to check comprehension orally, e.g. What's the name of the island?

Refer to Teacher's Notes Unit 1 page 99 for further examples of this type of question.

2 It is advisable to point out that 'the island' (para 1) refers to Bahamia, and 'it' (para 2) refers to Leeds before allowing the students to complete the text.

3 **Informal letter layout**

This is best demonstrated on the blackboard.

4 **Writing the letter**

This can be set for homework, but you should go through the advertisements beforehand and you may need to go through sample letters orally or on the blackboard, before allowing students to write their own, emphasising the information to be included.

Unit 3

Formal letters, Simple conjunctions, Writing a formal letter.

A Formal letters

1 Students should read the advertisement quickly in order to be able to answer the question. Explain that they can understand the general meaning without understanding every word.

2 **Addresses**

Ask students to look back at the headings for informal letters on page 16 and to tell you the difference between them and those for formal letters. Explain that we do not write our own name with our address, but we *do* write the receiver's name with his/her address.
Ask students to tell you the order in which the address is written.
The correct order is:
1 Name (when used)
2 Street number and name
3 Name of town
4 Name of county (not used with very big towns – London, Belfast, Edinburgh, etc. and often missed out now because of postcode)
5 Postcode

3 Punctuation

Point out that we use a capital letter for initials and in titles, names and letters of postcode, and a full stop after initials and abbreviations.

5 Formal letter layout

This can be explained on the blackboard before students read the letter and answer the focus questions. Go through the notes on page 19 and point out that 'Yours faithfully' is *only* used in letters with the beginnings given at **d** i and 'Yours sincerely' only with those at **d** ii.

B Conjunctions

1 You may help students to understand the use of these conjunctions by asking them to tell you which clause expresses a result ('so . . .'), which expresses a reason ('because . . .') and which phrase gives examples ('especially . . .').

Point out the use of 'and' between the two final items of a list, and the use of the comma to divide earlier items. 'But' is used in a position of contrast: in **d** a like is contrasted with a dislike.

2 Ask students to make up examples of their own illustrating the use of the conjunctions before allowing them to complete the exercise.

C Writing a formal letter

1 Students should do this exercise in pairs – they write out one letter each and check with their partner that each section has been used once only. Insist on correct layout of the letters.

2 Focus students' attention on the addresses. Ask who the person is writing to in each case, and ask for suggestions about the likely content of the letter. Talk about the details which might be included in such a letter. Students then work in groups of three to write the letters. It may be necessary to explain that this is not a jigsaw like the last exercise. Each letter is in the correct order. Point out that students should use both the factual information contained in the letters and the grammatical clues to complete the exercise. During the correction phase, ask students how they were able to work out the correct answers in order to focus their attention on the linking words in the letters.

3 Write your own letter

Go through the exercise orally before allowing students to complete the task. This may be set for homework.

Unit 4

Describing places, Combining adjectives, Compound words, Nouns as adjectives, Weather, Postcards.

A Describing places

1 Teach the word 'advertisement' and the abbreviated form of 'advert'. Ask students what kind of adjectives they find in an advertisement for a holiday resort, and write one or two phrases on the blackboard, such as 'beautiful beaches', 'sunny weather', etc. Underline the adjectives and then ask the students to do the same in the two texts. Draw up two lists on the board, one of positive and one of negative adjectives – students call out the adjectives.

2 This exercise may be done in teams or groups. The first group to find all the adjectives is the winner. Answers run vertically and horizontally.

3 This exercise is best completed individually and then checked in pairs.

B Combining adjectives

1 Point out that in English adjectives usually precede the noun. When two adjectives are followed by a noun they are usually not joined by the word 'and'. When two adjectives are not followed immediately by a noun, they are joined by 'and'. Point out the exception: colours.

3 The advertisement can be written for homework.

C Compound words

1 Students should work out for themselves that in compound words, such as 'family hotel', the second word names the object, and the first word is an adjective which gives more information about the object. Thus, a 'family hotel' is a hotel for families, a 'tennis ball' is a ball for playing tennis, and a 'ham sandwich' is a sandwich made with ham.

3 This activity can be done as a competition with a time limit – perhaps ten minutes. The winner is the pair or group producing the highest number of correct words. Beware of false friends such as 'tennis camp'. We play tennis on a 'tennis court' and go to a 'holiday camp' in the summer!

D Weather

1 This is a simple matching exercise.

2 Give the explanation on the blackboard with books closed. Write up the two sentences and explain or elicit:

> *It's raining* – now
> *It rains* – in general

Students complete i in pairs. They must decide whether the action is *now* or *in general* before choosing the correct answer. ii Describe today's weather to students, giving examples of the present continuous where applicable. Compare this with the *climate* and give examples of the climate of your region, using the present simple where possible. Go through four or five sentences of the text, asking whether students think they describe weather or climate. They should realise that the present continuous is used in the text about the weather while the present simple and adverbs of frequency are used in the text about climate.

3 This exercise may be set for homework.

E Postcards

1 This is a good moment to point out the division into paragraphs, with indentations for the beginning of each new paragraph. Tell students that this is an important feature of writing in English and that more work will be done on the subject later.

2 Explain to students that whichever place they choose to write about, they must make sure that their postcard is coherent and that all the choices they make are suitable for the place.

3 This exercise focuses on ellipsis. Point out that the shortened forms here are appropriate for use in writing informal postcards, while they would not be acceptable in letters. Students should realise that we can usually leave out articles, personal pronouns and auxiliary verbs when the meaning is not changed by their absence.

Unit 5

Places, Informal invitations and suggestions, Paragraphs.

A Places

1 Allow your students time to look at the map, then ask them questions to check their understanding, such as:
Where can you buy a table or a chair? (Living furniture)
Where can you eat? (Chinese restaurant, Burger bar, etc.)

2 i Refer to Teacher's Notes Unit 1 page 99 for further examples of this type of question. Point out the difference between 'near' and 'next to'.

2 ii Point out that in sentences **a, b, h** and **k**, the word 'it' refers back to the subject of the first sentence, that is, the first place mentioned in the sentence.

3 When students have completed this exercise, they can exchange their exercise books and correct each other's work.

4 **b** Give an example of this activity and allow students to guess where you are before you let them work in pairs.

B Informal invitations and suggestions

1 The questions are intended to focus attention on the poster as an introduction to this section.

2 Practise the invitations and refusals orally in class.

4 Demonstrate on the blackboard how to fill in the diary before allowing students to complete it for themselves.

5 Provide paper for this activity. Demonstrate the game carefully with one student before the class plays.

C Paragraphs

2 You should help students to see that it is easier to read something if the information is divided clearly into paragraphs. For example, in Letter A, you might have to read some parts twice because it is not clear that the writer has changed the subject. In the sentences '.... taking aspirin every four hours. How was the barbecue?', the change is too abrupt. If the writer was speaking, she would pause before beginning a new subject: when writing you can make this kind of pause by using paragraphs.

Point out that when we write in paragraphs we start a new line with an indentation for each new paragraph. Explain that writing in paragraphs is very important in English even though it may not be so important in the students' own language.

Unit 6

Instructions, Directions, Telephone messages.

A Instructions

2 In this exercise, students should work out from the text how to give instructions. They should work out that they use the INFINITIVE (without 'to') to give positive instruction and 'do not' + INFINITIVE (without 'to') to give a negative instruction. Point out that 'Do not' is the written form, and that in the spoken language it is usually abbreviated to 'Don't'. Explain that 'please' simply makes the instruction more polite; it does not turn it into a request.

3 Explain that at private schools, parents pay for their children's education, and many of them are single-sex schools. The sixth form is the class for students from the age of 16 to 18 and there are often some privileges such as a separate house not shared by the younger pupils.

4 This quiz can be very successful, but it must be demonstrated by the teacher first. You can use an examination as an example situation. (The word 'situation' will soon become clear to students if they don't understand.) Begin by saying, 'In this situation, do not smoke', pause to let the students make guesses. Continue until they guess correctly, with instructions like: 'Do not bring books into the room', 'Write in pen, not pencil'. Ask students to tell you what the instructions were, and write them on the board. Give another situation if necessary, e.g. 'You are on an escalator.' Elicit instructions from the students.

Remind students of the correct form used in giving instructions: INFINITIVE (without 'to'), 'do not' + INFINITIVE (without 'to'), before allowing them to think of their own situations.

B Directions

1 Make sure your students understand that we use 'Go straight on' without an object and 'Go straight along ...' with an object (e.g. 'Go straight along Market Street'). Watch out for mistakes like 'Go straight on Redham Street'. Use diagrams **c, d,** and **e** on page 48 to emphasise the difference.

The other language items in this section can be presented as set forms. Check that students use the correct prepositions in these forms:

Turn left *into* Redham Road
Come *out of* the bus station.
At the traffic lights turn left.

2 Explain to the students that they do not need to understand the whole letter – it is sufficient for them to complete the task.

4 An alternative to this would be to use the same exercise, but using a plan of the students' own town, or the town where they are studying. In this case you should make sure each pair has a map.

Unit 7

Writing about the past, Giving more information, Sending a telex.

A Writing about the past

In these sections we look at the different ways of writing about the past. We assume that the forms of the simple past and the past continuous are not new to students. However, we expect that work is still needed on the different uses of these tenses.

B Ordering events

1 Point out that the two expressions in **a** and the two in **b** are alternative ways of saying the same thing. Both are correct.

2 Before students complete the exercise, check that they understand the verbs in the list below the illustrations, and know the past tenses.

C Description and action in the past

1 Refer students back to the letter in A 1 and point out that 'I was sunbathing' describes the situation (what was happening at the time), while 'he arrived' describes the action.

3 Ask the students where they think the scene takes place, and why. For example:

> What were the two men at the table doing?
> What was the barmaid doing?
> What was the pianist doing?
> What was the man at the bar doing?

4 a Allow students to complete their description of the situation and then compare them with other versions.

b Pre-teach verbs such as : Shoot (shot) someone, fall (fell) down, die (died), hide (hid), run (ran) away. Allow students to discuss what happened before they complete the exercise.

7 It is advisable to demonstrate the time-line on the blackboard by drawing it one stage at a time, as follows:

Stage 1: _____
 T I M E

The line represents time passing.

Stage 2:
 NOW
 _____
 T I M E

The vertical line indicates NOW – the space before the arrow indicates past time.

Stage 3:
 NOW
 _____
 T I M E

The vertical lines represent precise moments in the past, and actions that happened at these times.

Stage 4:
 NOW
 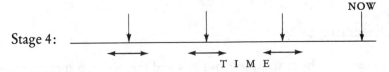
 T I M E

The horizontal lines represent what was happening at the time of the actions (the general situation).

Not all students will find time-lines easy to understand, but many will find them a great help in remembering how tenses are used in English.
Point out that 'while' is often followed by the past continuous, although 'when' can also be used in this position.

D Giving more information

At this stage, we do not discuss contact clauses or the relative pronoun 'that'. Students should be able to write satisfactory English at this level without these additional forms.

E Sending a telex

It is becoming increasingly important to be able to read and write telexes in English. Explain to students that it is not essential to use abbreviations in telexes. A clear message written in short, simple sentences is always preferable to complicated sentences or incorrect abbreviations. The most important thing is to get the message across in a way that can be understood.

Unit 8

Curriculum vitae, Writing a curriculum vitae, Letters of application for a job, Writing about past experience, Sending a telegram.

A Curriculum vitae

The c.v. contains a good deal of vocabulary which cannot be guessed from context and which should be explained.
You should also explain the following:

G.C.E. General Certificate of Education (the English State secondary school exam until 1988, when it was replaced by the GCSE, General Certificate of Secondary Education).
O level Ordinary Level, usually taken at 15 or 16.
A level Advanced Level, usually taken at 18.
B.Sc. Bachelor of Science (a general title for any science degree).

B Writing a curriculum vitae

1 You should go through the description on how to write a c.v. and refer to Richard's c.v. for clarification. You may like to point out that more and more people are using the American style c.v. where work experience is given before education.

2 Pre-teach 'store' and 'boss' and make sure the students know the word 'employer' is a formal equivalent of 'boss', for use on the c.v.

4 Students should write their own c.v., in class or for homework. This will clearly be a short exercise among a group of 15-year-olds! To make it more meaningful, ask them to write a c.v. for their favourite pop star/sports personality, etc. (You could take in a brief biography cut out from a magazine as a source of information.) Alternatively, let them invent a personality.

5 The aim of this exercise is to practise, in a controlled way, the transfer of information from the c.v. to the letter. Students should refer both to Richard's letter on page 65 and Lisa's c.v., and fill in the spaces.

C Writing about the past

1 This section contrasts the present perfect simple with the past simple, with particular reference to applying for jobs: previous jobs, length of experience etc.

It is a good idea to introduce the section with books closed, as students must fully understand these time-lines. Write the four examples on the board and ask students for explanations of the different forms of the verbs. Then draw each time-line on the board in stages (see Teacher's Notes Unit 7, C7, page 110). Students should be asked after each stage what the drawing represents.

You may find students are inclined to use the present simple instead of the present perfect here (perhaps because their own language uses the present), even when they have understood the concept – so extra practice may be necessary.

3 In this exercise, students choose between the simple present, simple past and the present perfect.

4 Make sure the students understand all the vocabulary and the concepts on the time-line. Explain the principle again if necessary. You may like to ask them to make up sentences for the different ideas and write them up on the board.

Before starting the exercise, make sure the students are familiar, with the form 'been to', otherwise they will probably write 'gone to'. Explain the difference if necessary:

been to = He has gone *and* returned.
gone to = He has gone and *not* returned.

5 **Personal time-lines**

Before they do this exercise, ask the students for examples of what they might want to write. If you do not know your students well, or they do not want to reveal information about themselves, make it clear that they can invent things. When they have completed the exercise, read out a few examples and see if the students can guess who wrote the text.

D Writing a letter of application for a job

1 Go over the plan with the students. At this level, you can introduce a number of 'fixed phrases', such as 'I am writing to apply for a position as ... with your company', 'I would be grateful if you would consider my application' and 'As you will see from my curriculum vitae ...' without going into them in detail. Stress that the letter should be well laid-out, and in clear paragraphs.

2 Students should read the two advertisements in class, checking vocabulary with the teacher or dictionary. They should choose the one they would rather apply for. The letter can be written in class or for homework.

E Sending a telegram

3 It is important for the students to realise that most pronouns, auxiliary verbs and prepositions are omitted unless the meaning is not clear without them. Point out 'meet *me*'. This pronoun makes it clear that it is Jennie who is arriving.

5 This text can be reduced to about sixteen words. For example:

> Sorry can't meet you Monday.
> Working at Club. Suggest
> take taxi. Please bring
> blue sunglasses. Tony.

7 Discuss with students on what occasions they could send telegrams and what they could say in them e.g. Congratulations, Happy Birthday, Good luck, etc.

8 In this exercise, students are given practice in recognising appropriate telegram language. Where appropriate students may practise writing this language by sending 'telegrams' to other students in the class. However, students should not be expected to use this language actively at this stage.

Students should realise that the person who is sending the telegram has the name at the end of the telegram and the person to whom the message is addressed is at the beginning of the telegram.

Unit 9

Looking towards the future, Reports, Conjunctions, Comparatives, Ordering your ideas – marking words, Writing a report.

A Looking towards the future

2 The use of 'going to' as a future auxiliary can cause problems. You should explain clearly to your students that, in the first sentence, 'go' is the main verb and Jennie is talking about the present. She is literally going (travelling) to visit her husband at the moment of speaking. In the second sentence the main verb is 'work'. 'Going to' is used as an auxiliary verb to show that it is Richard's intention in the future to work there for one or two months.

3 Tell students to write these lists in their exercise books.

4 Build up the time-line on the board gradually before students see it in their books. (See Teacher's Notes C7, page 110.)

6 Note that here we are using spoken language, so the students can use abbreviated forms.

B Reports

1 It is important to go over the notes and check that students understand all the adjectives.

C Conjunctions

Tell the students that by using conjunctions they can make complex sentences to express complex ideas. They must realise how the conjunctions work, as translation is often misleading.

1 'But', 'Although' and 'However' are used to join contrasting ideas, often a positive and a negative idea.
BUT is usually found in the middle of the sentence linking the two ideas.
ALTHOUGH can be found at the beginning or in the middle of the sentence.
HOWEVER is usually found at the beginning of the sentence containing the contrasting idea. It will therefore usually start with a capital letter. It can also be found at the end of a sentence.

4 and 5 After completing the exercises point out how the sentences with 'because' can be re-written with 'so':
e.g. *The Sudan is near the Equator so the weather is hot.*
and vice versa
e.g. *I'm going to stay at home because I don't feel very well this morning.*

D Comparatives

2 Check that students know how to count syllables in English. Demonstrate how to count them according to the number of beats in a word.
e.g. young = 1   hap-py = 2   dan-ger-ous = 3
Then check through the rules in the table, giving other examples of each category as necessary.

Point out the two-syllable adjectives which do not end in '-y' but nevertheless form the comparative in '-er', such as 'clever-er', 'quiet-er'. These are exceptions to the general rule and students should learn them. Beware, however, as 'quieter' occurs in the next exercise!

5 The differences should be clear from the pictures. Point out that in English 'not as .... as' is frequently preferred to the comparative + 'than'. So we say:

   Betty is not as tall as Laura
rather than:

   Betty is shorter than Laura.

Remind students of the grammatical rules if necessary:
'not as' + ADJECTIVE + 'as'   'as + tall + as'
   COMPARATIVE + 'than'   'taller than'

E Ordering your ideas – marking words

1 Note that 'first' and 'firstly', 'second' and 'secondly' are
  synonymous. 'plc' stands for 'public limited company'.

F Writing a report

1 Go through the lists before students start making notes. 'Work'
  means what they actually have to do. 'Work/school life' means the
  general atmosphere of these places. Check that they understand the
  adjectives. You can tell them that the lists are only a guide to help
  them, and if they want to discuss something else or use other
  adjectives, they should do so.

Unit 10

Formal invitations, Narrative, Consolidation.

A Formal invitations

2 The language used in formal invitations is conventional and includes
  set phrases which should only be used in these contexts. Students
  should be able to recognise and reply to such language.

  Formal invitations are usually printed cards or letters, used to invite
  people to formal occasions – weddings, conferences, formal dinner
  parties, etc. They often include 'R.S.V.P.', which is an abbreviation for
  the French 'Répondez s'il vous plaît'. This convention dates from the
  period when French was the language used in international social
  circles and means that a reply is expected.

  Informal invitations (see Unit 5 pages 36–9) are usually informal
  letters or notes between friends to tell them about informal and
  formal occasions. Sometimes an informal letter is sent to invite
  someone to a formal event, and then a formal invitation follows.

3 Guests at a charity lunch pay for their meal; profits are given to
  charity.

4 Explain that the choice of concluding phrase will depend on the
  context, e.g. 'I hope you have a good time' will be appropriate for a
  wedding invitation, 'I hope to see you soon' for friends or
  acquaintances.

6 Make sure that an invitation is written for every student, so that every
  student will be able to write a reply. If necessary tell them who to
  write to. It is perhaps better for this exercise if the person they invite
  is not sitting next to them.

B Narrative

1 This exercise is a consolidation of work already done on tenses. Before starting the exercise, point out to students the work done on time-lines in Units 7, 8 and 9. Make sure that students understand that the thick line represents time passing, the vertical arrows represent points in time, and the shorter horizontal lines represent either specified or unspecified periods of time.

2 This is a form of revision. At this point you may want to revise the grammatical forms as well as the use of the tenses. This will depend on the level of the class.

4 For this exercise you should give the students a piece of paper. Make sure they write 'you' questions – i.e. not questions with 'he' or 'she' because other students must be able to answer them. You may need to revise the grammar of question-forming before doing this exercise.

When they have finished their questions, put the papers in a 'post-box' i.e. a large box (or any suitable container), and mix them up. Then let each student take one piece of paper and write the answers to the questions on it.

Read out a few to the whole class when they have finished.

C Consolidation

This task gives practice in making notes which will then be used in the final writing task C2, which gives the student the opportunity to write fairly extensively and to choose one of several styles – diary, letter or report – all of which have been practised before. If your class finds it difficult, or does not want to write about their real lives, they may invent something. Make sure they understand which tenses they will probably but not necessarily need to use in the different sections. Remember this is only a guideline. Other tenses such as the present tense may be used, depending on what students want to say:

a Simple Past – for events that take place at a specific time in the past.
b Past Continuous – for descriptions of situations.
c Present Perfect – What has happened since a past time.
d 'Going to' – for future intentions.

2 Provide paper for this exercise and make sure students do not write their names on the paper as another student must guess who wrote it afterwards.

3 When they have finished writing, take the papers in and give each student a paper that someone else has written. They should read it and guess who wrote it.

4 Ask a few students quickly to tell the class who they think wrote the paper and why.

5 See notes for Consequences, Unit 5, part B5. The principle is the same, but the language students will use is different – to practise different things. Here we are practising the uses of tenses.

ANSWERS

ANSWERS

Unit 1

A

3 a (1)student (2)Scotland (3)28 (4)married
  (5)Bradford
  (6)Glantree (7)9th August 19––
  (8)Bradford Theatre Group (9)theatre,
  cinema and reading.

  b (1)23 (2)bicycle mechanic (3)Leeds
  (4)Roundhay Health Club
  (5)Dr Finsworth (6)swimming, tennis
  and skiing
  (7)travelling and cooking

C

4 Hello. I'm Anne Marshall. I live in Leeds, a
  large town in the north of England near
  Bradford. I like travelling, and on Saturday
  I'm going to London with Tony. Who is
  Tony? Well, he's my Scottish friend. He's
  married and his wife's name is Jennie.

Unit 2

A

1 a Bridlingpool   b Redham
  c White Sands   d York Town
  e Bahamia   f Mount Gunne
  g Lake Bader   h St. Peter's   i Pandora

2 b This is Redham, a small town near the
    capital.
  c This is White Sands, a sandy beach on the
    south coast.
  d This is York Town, the capital of
    Bahamia.
  e This is Bahamia, a holiday island in the
    Irenian Sea.
  f This is Mount Gunne, an important
    skiing centre.
  g This is Lake Bader, a popular
    wind-surfing centre north of York
    Town.
  h This is St Peter's, a winter holiday resort
    south of Mount Gunne.
  i This is Pandora, a seaside town in the
    east of the island.

3 Edinburgh is **the** capital of Scotland. The
  Highlands are – mountains **in** the north of
  Scotland. Liverpool is **a** famous port **on** the
  west coast of England and Hoylake is **a**
  seaside town south **of** Liverpool. Leeds is
  an industrial city **in** the north of England.
  London is **the** capital of England and
  Croydon is a town **near** London. The Isle
  of Wight is **an** island in the English Channel.

B

1 b King Peter is **56**. He is married and has
    four children.
  c **Princess** Sally is **22**. She is **single** and has
    no children.
  d **Princess** Elaine is **30**. She is married and
    has **two** children, **a boy and a girl**.
  e **Queen** Christine is **54**. She is married and
    has **four** children.
  f **Prince** David is **33**. He is a widower and
    has **one child, a girl**.
  g **Prince** Gavin is **14**. He is **single** and has
    no children.

D

1 a From Anne   b In Leeds   c To Gary
  d She wants to exchange letters and visits.

2 Anne Marshall is from **Leeds**, a **large** town **in** the **north** of England. She likes **Bahamia** very much. She was there on holiday last **summer**.

She is **23** years old and she is **single**. She works as a **bicycle mechanic** for **Northern Bikes,** a small company near her **house**.

She is writing to **Gary**, who lives in **Pandora**, a seaside town on the northeast coast of **Bahamia**.

Unit 3

A

4 a Miss F. Wood   **b** Mr L. Thompson
   3 Brown Street   53 Ashcroft Rd
   Exworth   Edinburgh E5
   Essex
   E24 5SW

  c Mr L. Price   **d** Mrs B. Stanton
   8 Saville Street   23 Heartshead St
   London W14   Birmingham B15

  e Ms M. Grey
   Denwood Holidays
   8 Chester St
   Glasgow G3

5 a From Ben Smith **b** To Mr J. Hines
  c Details of Balmy Holidays and an application form.

B

2 I love buying clothes, **especially** in the sales, **so** last week I went into town to look at the shops. I haven't got much money **because** I'm only a student. I wanted to buy some leather trousers **and** a jacket, **but** I didn't have enough money **so** I bought a pair of jeans instead.

3 Dear Mr and Mrs Wilcox,
I am very happy that you can come to visit us in August **and** I would like to tell you something about my town.

The weather here in August is usually very good, **but** bring a warm jumper or jacket with you **because** it is sometimes cool in the evenings.

I know that you like going to the theatre and to the opera, **so** I have booked tickets for the performance of 'Aida' on 4th August. The opera starts at 9.00 in the evening. **Because** there are a lot of people **and** the seats do not have numbers we must arrive very early.

I know that you will like the monuments in Verona, **especially** the Arena and the Roman theatre.

There are a lot of good restaurants **and** cafés in Verona **and** we can try some of the local dishes. I am sure you will like our food, **especially** the pasta dishes **and** the fruit ice-cream.

Please write to me soon **and** tell me what time you are arriving in Verona.

With best wishes,

Antonia Gelli

C

1 (Suggested answers):

3 Brown Street
Exworth
Essex E24 54W

Mr L. Price
Elegant Fashions
53 Ashcroft Street
London W14   8th October 19––

Dear Mr Price,

I am very interested in your fashions, especially the winter dresses section, so could you please send me a catalogue with more details and an order form.

I am looking forward to hearing from you.

Yours sincerely,

10 Birch Grove
Retford
Notts.
DN33 WB1

The Box Office
The Royal Opera House
Coventry Street
Liverpool
Merseyside L28   16th April 19––

Dear Sir or Madam,

I love classical music, especially Mozart and Haydn, and I am very interested in your programme this year. I would like to see as many productions as possible, so could you please send me an application form for the season ticket that you provide.

I look forward to hearing from you.

Yours faithfully,

2 (Suggested answers):

16 The Avenue
Staines
Middlesex

Scottish Tourist Board
1 Waverley Street
Edinburgh   16th March 19––

Dear Sir or Madam,

I am writing to ask about the tours of the Scottish lochs and Highlands in August 19–– My husband and I will be in Edinburgh for the first three weeks in August. I enclose a s.a.e. for your reply.

Would you please also send me some information about the Edinburgh festival. I look forward to hearing from you.

Yours faithfully,

247 Station Road
St Albans
Herts.
AL3 5DG

Hotel Dolomiten
Samnaun
Switzerland   22nd December 19––

Dear Sir or Madam,

I am writing to confirm my telephone booking for two single rooms with bathroom from 9th to 15th March 19––. We hope to arrive at the hotel on Sunday afternoon at about 5.00. I enclose a cheque for the deposit of £50.

Would you please send me a receipt for the £50.00. I look forward to hearing from you.

Yours faithfully,

42A Sydney St
London N8

Box Office
Palace Theatre
Strand Street
London WC1   19th January 19––

Dear Sirs,

I would like to confirm my reservation for three tickets for the performance of 'Othello' on Saturday 8th March. Would you please also send me two £7 tickets for 'Cats' on 17th March. I enclose a postal order for £35 (5 × £7).

Would you please send me the tickets to the above address. I look forward to hearing from you.

Yours faithfully,

Unit 4

A

2 interesting, great, horrible, terrible, awful, incredible, quiet, excellent, fantastic, disgusting, greasy.

3 any sensible answers accepted.

B

2 **a** small and dirty
  b beautiful little
  c quiet friendly
  d large industrial
  e noisy and exciting
  f exciting historic
  g large interesting
  h horrible expensive
  i small and dark
  j wonderful little ... lovely blue

C

1 **a** i **b** i **c** ii

2 **b** a night-club **c** a bicycle mechanic
  d a record player **e** a coffee cup
  f a wine-glass

D

1 **a** It's snowing. **b** It's sunny.
  c It's raining. **d** It's cloudy and cold.
  e It's windy. **f** It's foggy.
  g It's hot.

2 i 1 b 2 a 3 a 4 b 5 b 6 a 7 b
  8 b 9 a 10 b

  ii *Text 1*: 1, 3, 5, 7, 8, 11, 12, 15
  Text 2: 2, 4, 6, 9, 10, 13, 14

E

1 **a** Tony (Anne's having a shower!).
  b Not much – it's a bit boring.
  c In the shower.
  d Two.
  e Balmy Holiday Club – because they haven't got much money left.

2 A – 4 B – 2 C – 5 D – 3 E – 1.

4 **b** The ... **c** I'm ... **d** We ...
  e We ... **f** We're ... **g** because it's too hot **h** I (We) ...

5 Exclude:
  b I'm **c** The **d** I **e** because → cos
  f I **g** It's **h** I'll

Unit 5

A

2 ii **a** next to ... opposite ... on the corner of
  b opposite ... next to ... on the corner of
  c between
  d next to ... opposite
  e next to/on the left of
  f next to ... opposite/near
  g next to ... opposite
  h between ... opposite/near ... next to/on the right of
  i next to
  j opposite
  k between ... opposite
  l on the corner of

  (These are suggested answers, but do not cover all the possibilities.)

B

1 **a** hamburgers and sausages **b** No charge
  c £2 **d** 25th July **e** 8.00 p.m.
  f listen to music, eat, drink, dance etc.

3 Let's ⬜6⬜, Would you like to ⬜7⬜, shall we meet ⬜8⬜, I'm afraid I'm ⬜9⬜, Would you like to go? ⬜1⬜, How about ⬜4⬜, Why don't we ⬜10⬜, Would you like to go ⬜3⬜, I'd like to ⬜5⬜, I can't because ⬜2⬜.

C

1 a She has a bad cold. **b** No
c 'Time for Tea'
d She liked the photography but not the story.
e Italian

2 A has no paragraphs

3 Suggested titles: **1** Greetings
2 Barbecue **3** Tony **4** Gary
5 Invitation to dinner

5 There are no paragraphs.
a – 5 **b** – 2 **c** – 1 **d** – 3 **e** – 4

Division of paragraphs (suggested answer):
//How ...... expensive.//Then .... love it here.//The club ..... great!//White .....
Street.//Anyway .... ask?//

Unit 6

A

1 a T **b** T **c** F **d** T **e** T **f** F **g** F

B

3 b Odeon cinema – F **c** police station – E
d private beach – B **e** Feathers Club – D
f Sea View Hotel – A

C

1 a Anne **b** Tony
c Anne must meet him at Reception at 7.30 p.m.

3 (Suggested answer) Elaine, Julie phoned. She can't meet you this afternoon because she has to go to Leeds. She can meet you tomorrow for a drink at Mantovani's. Please phone her tomorrow morning at the office.
     Peter

Unit 7

A

1 Suggested answers:
a No
b Yes, very much.
c No, she hates it.
d She wanted to go back to England.

2

Regular		Irregular	
wash	washed	is	was
dance	danced	meet	met
talk	talked	give	gave
arrive	arrived	make	made
prepare	prepared	eat	ate
tidy	tidied	sweep	swept
want	wanted	drink	drank
invite	invited	say	said

B

2 (Suggested answers)
a She put on suntan lotion before she sunbathed.
     She put on suntan lotion before sunbathing.
b After eating her meal, she went to the disco.
     After she ate her meal, she went to the disco.
c He cleaned his teeth before he went to bed.
     He cleaned his teeth before going to bed.

d Before the plane took off, he bought a
book.
Before taking off, he bought a book.

C

2 Column One –
Situations: **b** were closing,
c were playing, **d** were singing.

Column Two –
Actions that continue the story: **a** came,
b lit, **c** walked, **d** waited.

6 went ... arrived ... saw ... were talking ...
waited/was waiting ... looked ... wore/was
wearing ... remembered ... said ... replied
... met ... broke ... drank ...

7 a when, **b** when/while, **c** while/when,
d when, **e** while/when, **f** when.

8 a waiting ... met
b arrived ... when/while ... was having ...
c reading when ... rang
d saw ... when/while ... was walking
down/along the ...
Other answers are possible.

D

2 a where **b** who **c** where **d** which
e who **f** which **g** which **h** where
i who **j** which

3 (1)e (2)c/f (3)f/c (4)g (5)a (6)d
(7)b

E

2 a 2 **b** 1 **c** 3 **d** 6 **e** 4 **f** 5

3 Suggested answers:
a Director of holiday camp in Pandora.
b He wants to employ another assistant for
the camp.
c Free answer.
d Can I take on another assistant ... etc.

4 (Suggested answer)
5839321 PARIS P

459760 BALMY J

ATTN: JOURDAIN

TKS FOR YR TLX. I HAVE A FRIEND OF ANNE
AND TONY COMING FOR AN INTERVIEW.
I WILL ADVISE YOU ABOUT THE RESULT.
ANNE MARSHALL AND TONY
FIELD ARE DOING VERY WELL
AND I AM VERY HAPPY WITH THEIR
WORK.
OUR OLD BAR IS TOO SMALL NOW
THE CAMP IS FULL. PLS CAN I OPEN
ANOTHER ONE?
I AWAIT YOUR REPLY ASAP.
TKS. RGDS
JIM ELSWORTHY
DIRECTOR/PANDORA BALMY
HOLIDAYS

459760 BALMY J
5839321 PARIS P

Unit 8

A

2 Richard has worked in a holiday camp, not
in a hotel. He has not worked as a shop
assistant. He left Polytechnic, not
University, in 1982. Then he worked for
three years as a computer programmer in
Luton. From 1986 to 1987 he was a travel
guide in Athens. Since 1987, he has worked
as a photographer. He has been a qualified
tennis instructor since 1985, and has had his
driving licence since 1978. He plays
football, not rugby.

B

3 Title: Mrs

Address: 128a Station Street, Perth,
Scotland. Tel: 0738-55462
Date of Birth: 4.4.65   O levels: French,
English, Maths, Statistics

Experience:
1981–1985   . . .
1985–1986   Trainee Store Manager,
MacVie's, Perth
1986–present   Store Manager, Bloxham's,
Stirling

Languages: French
Hobbies: Water-skiing, swimming
References: Mr Iain McDonald, 66 The
Rise, Perth, Scotland
Mrs Mary Dalton, Area Manager,
Bloxham's Stores, Bloxham House, High
Street, Stirling, Scotland.

5 128a Station Street, . . . Perth, . . . Sir(s) . . .
apply . . . from my curriculum vitae . . . 1981
. . . Superstores . . . 1985 . . . MacVie's . . .
1986 . . . Stirling . . . O levels . . . Maths . . .
French . . . water-skiing and swimming . . .
faithfully

C

3 **a** lived **b** have had **c** arrived
d has worked **e** went
f stayed **g** have lived **h** worked

4 . . . has lived . . . moved . . . has worked . . .
worked . . . has played . . . has been

E

2 **b** am, **c** on, **d** at, **e** at, **f** airport,
g on, **h** love

4 **a** 7, **b** 4, **c** 5, **d** 3, **e** 1 **f** 2, **g** 6.

5 (Suggested answer)
Sorry can't meet you Monday. Working at
Club. Suggest take taxi to Club. Please
bring blue sunglasses. Tony.

8 **a** Elspeth, **b** Tim Ainsley,
c Jack and Liz, **d** Mary, **e** Tony,
f Grandma, **g** P. Brownwell

Unit 9

A

1 **a** Jennie is Tony's wife. Richard is Tony's
friend.
b On a plane going to Bahamia.
c Richard is going to work at the Holiday
Club for one or two months, then he's
going to travel for the rest of the year.
Next year, he's going to look for a more
permanent job. Jennie's going to stay
with Tony for a week, then she's going to
go skiing on Mount Gunne.

3 Richard's intentions:
b He's going to travel for the rest of the
year.
c He's going to look for a more permanent
job.

Jennie's intentions
a She's going to Bahamia to stay with
Tony.
b She's going to stay in White Sands for a
week.
c She's going to go skiing on Mount
Gunne.

B

1 **a** True **b** True **c** False **d** True
e False

2 hard . . . popular . . . punctual . . . late . . .
dreamer . . . shy . . . well . . . better . . .
problem . . . using . . . three . . . cold . . . dirty
. . . trees . . . white . . .

C

2 Positive:

b There were some lovely shops.
c You organised wonderful disco parties.
d The cocktails were incredible.
e The bedroom had a lovely balcony.

Negative:

b The waiters were sometimes rude.
c The bed was very hard.
d The souvenirs were expensive.
e The mosquitoes were a pest.
f It was very noisy at night.

3 a The club was wonderful, but the weather was not very good.
b You organised wonderful disco parties, but it was very noisy at night.
c The waiters were sometimes rude, although the cocktails were incredible.
d There were some lovely shops although the souvenirs were expensive.
e The bedroom had a lovely balcony. However, the bed was very hard.
f You kept the pool lovely and warm although the mosquitoes were a pest. Other answers are possible.

D

1 *Hilda:* **b** very happy, **c** very dark hair, **d** good cook, **e** young, **f** bad at sport, **g** very popular, **h** always very late, **i** hard-working

Mavis: **b** happy, **c** dark hair, **d** very good cook, **e** young, **f** very bad at sport, **g** popular, **h** often late, **i** very hard-working.
(Note that these are suggested answers. The exercise is designed to provoke discussion of the meaning of the adjectives.)

D

2 b Mavis is fatter than Hilda.
c Mavis is happier than Hilda.
d Hilda is always later than Mavis.
e Hilda is more popular than Mavis.
f Mavis is a better cook than Hilda./ Mavis is worse at sport than Hilda.

3 more popular ... more confident ... later ... more punctual ... happier ... quieter ... better.

5 a than **b** as **c** as **d** than **e** as **f** as **g** than **h** as **i** as **j** than **k** as **l** as **m** than

E

1 a They have a young, dynamic Managing Director.
b They have introduced new technology in all parts of the company.
c They have a permanent contract with the Bahamian government.

Unit 10

A

1 a Peter Robinson **b** Anne Marshall and Gary Suarez **c** Anne Marshall's father **d** at St James's Church, Highgate on Saturday 12th December at 3.00 pm. **e** Répondez s'il vous plaît

2 a is formal and **b** is informal

3 a 5, **b** 3, **c** 4, **d** 2, **e** 1.

4 a says 'Yes' and **b** says 'No'.

5 Dear Mr and Mrs Folkes, Thank you very much for your invitation. I am afraid I will not be able to come as I am going to Paris that weekend. With best wishes, Yours, Richard Wilton.

B

2 2 E, 3 C, 4 D, 5 B, 6 G, 7 F,
8 I, 9 H, 10 J.

5 was ... were ... lived ... knew ... had ...
went ... did not like ... was ... got ... was
studying ... came ... told ... went ... was
... was living ... told ... told ... was
studying ... was writing ... was ... was ...
wanted ... had ... could not ... saw ...
wanted ... agreed ... was ... found ... have
worked ... have used ... have saved ... do
not like ... is not ... am going to move ...
am going to study ...